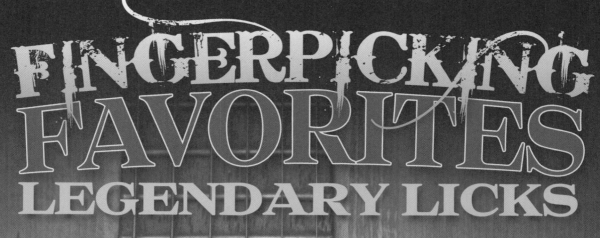

FINGERPICKING FAVORITES
LEGENDARY LICKS

BY TOBY WINE

Recording Credit:
Doug Boduch, guitar

Cherry Lane Music Company
Director of Publications: Mark Phillips

ISBN 978-1-60378-384-2

Copyright © 2012 Cherry Lane Music Company
International Copyright Secured   All Rights Reserved

The music, text, design and graphics in this publication are protected by copyright law. Any duplication or transmission,
by any means, electronic, mechanical, photocopying, recording or otherwise, is an infringement of copyright.

Visit our website at www.cherrylaneprint.com

Contents

About the Author

Toby Wine is a native New Yorker and a freelance guitarist, composer, arranger, and educator. He is a graduate of the Manhattan School of Music, where he studied composition with Manny Albam and Edward Green. Toby has performed with Philip Harper (of the Harper Brothers and Art Blakey's Jazz Messengers), Bob Mover, Ari Ambrose, Michael and Carolyn Leonhart (of Steely Dan), Peter Hartmann, Ian Hendrickson-Smith (of Sharon Jones and the Dap-Kings), Melee, Saycon (*Fela!*), Nakia Henry, and the Harlem-based rock band Kojomodibo Sun, among others. His arrangements and compositions can be heard on recordings by Tobias Gebb and Unit Seven (*Free at Last*), Phillip Harper (*Soulful Sin, The Thirteenth Moon*, Muse Records), Ari Ambrose (*Early Song*, Steeplechase), and Ian Hendrickson-Smith (*Up in Smoke*, Sharp Nine). Toby leads his own trio and septet, does studio sessions, and works as a sideman with a variety of tri-state area bandleaders. He spent four years as the music librarian for the Carnegie Hall Jazz band and is currently an instructor at the Church Street School for Music and Art in Tribeca. He is the author of numerous Cherry Lane publications, including *The Art of Texas Blues, 150 Cool Jazz Licks in Tab, Bluesmasters by the Bar, John Mayer: Legendary Licks, Steely Dan: Legendary Licks,* and *Derek Trucks: Legendary Licks.*

Acknowledgments

Many thanks are due to Cherry Lane's fearless leaders, John Stix and Mark Phillips, and to Susan Poliniak, for her insight, guidance, and continued support over the last decade. Thanks as well to my parents, Rosemary and Jerry, and to Christina, Bibi, Bob, Jack Wein, Jack Shniedman, Noah, Enid, Mover, Humph (R.I.P.), fellow author Karl Kaminski, and all the great teachers (and students) I've had. I've learned so much from all of you.

Introduction

Fingerpicking is both an art and a technical approach to the guitar. It transcends the boundaries of style and offers the skilled practitioner a host of possibilities unavailable to the pick-only player. In some respects, the fingerstyle guitarist enjoys a more intimate relationship with the instrument than that of the flatpicker, who is by definition always one degree removed from the strings by a small wedge of plastic. This heightened sense of intimacy is often reflected in both tone and artistic temperament. However, the technique is not solely the province of sensitive folkies and coffeehouse confessors. In the pages of *Fingerpicking Favorites*, we'll examine the work of folk pioneers (Simon & Garfunkel; Crosby, Stills & Nash; and James Taylor), '70s supergroups (Kansas and Fleetwood Mac), English bluesmen (Eric Clapton), timeless iconoclasts (Bob Dylan), southern gentleman (Doc Watson and Mason Williams), southern rockers (Lynyrd Skynyrd), as well as mega-pop stars of both yesterday and today (the Beatles and John Mayer). Each song by these enduring artists is broken down and explained, with standard notation, tablature, and detailed instructions for both fretting and fingerpicking hands. Whether you're a newcomer learning your way around the instrument, an experienced player looking to diversify your skill set, or simply a fan of the songs included, *Fingerpicking Favorites* will shine a light on this time-honored tradition and get you started on the road to your own deeper and more intimate relationship with the guitar.

Fingerpicking Techniques: A Crash Course

Playing the guitar without a pick is actually much less intuitive than it may initially appear to be. One may go about it willy-nilly, using whatever technique or system one chooses in a given situation—or not use any system at all—but as in much of life, a logical and ordered approach will yield a better result (or, at the very least, get you there in a much more efficient manner). A haphazard attitude towards fingerpicking (or any picking, for that matter) may yield acceptable results at a slow tempo in the privacy of your practice room but fall apart badly when attempted at full speed and in "real time," when you can't stop and start to fix any mistakes. In this chapter, we'll take a look at some of the most common fingerpicking techniques as we prepare to tackle the songs that follow. Individual lessons for each tune will also delve into their specific technical demands and help you avoid any pitfalls along the way. Note that, throughout this book, the picking fingers of the right hand will be referred to by their "common" names: thumb, index finger, middle finger, ring finger, and pinky. The left hand fingers will be numbered 1st (index), 2nd (middle), 3rd (ring), and 4th (pinky). In a few instances, the left-hand thumb will be required to play bass notes on the low E string by hooking over the top of the neck, but will not be assigned a number.

There are countless ways to use your fingers to pluck the strings, many of which are unique to individual players or to a small segment of the guitar playing population. John Mayer, whose song "The Heart of Life" is explored later in these pages, has more than one unusual technique, including a simultaneous thumb pluck and index-finger strum combination move that takes a bit of practice to get a handle on. The hugely influential jazz guitarist Wes Montgomery used his thumb much like a pick while liberally hammering on and pulling off with the left hand to fashion high-speed single-note solos. The great country guitarists of the Nashville studio scene are known for "hybrid" picking styles in which a pick is grasped by the thumb and index finger and used to pluck low notes while the middle and ring fingers grab higher notes with bare fingertips. And of course, classically trained guitarists are highly systematic in their right-hand approach as necessitated by their diverse and often difficult repertoire.

Rather than worry needlessly about this vast array of techniques, let's instead narrow things down to the essentials you will encounter in the songs to follow. To begin with, whether you sit or stand while you play, make sure that your right hand is in a comfortable position, with all six strings easily accessible. The first exercise uses a basic D chord in the left hand and "assigns" each of the four strings in the chord to a different right-hand finger. The thumb will pluck the D string, and the index, middle, and ring fingers will pluck the G, B, and high E strings, respectively. The right-hand pinky is almost never used in fingerstyle playing. The thumb should be roughly parallel to the strings and pluck in a downward motion, while the other fingers should curl inward towards the palm as they pick.

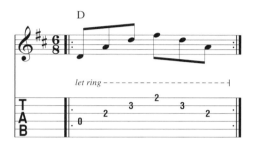

Applying a similar pattern to a chord progression is easy, although if the other chords (in this instance) have more than four notes, you will have some choices to make. In the following exercise, stay with the four strings/four fingers approach, but skip the A string entirely during the G chord. The B that would normally be played on its 2nd fret is played in the upper octave on the open B string anyway. You'll need to shift your index, middle, and fing fingers down to the D, G, and B strings, respectively, for the G and A chords. Repeat this and all other exercises as many times as you need to until they're comfortably under your fingers.

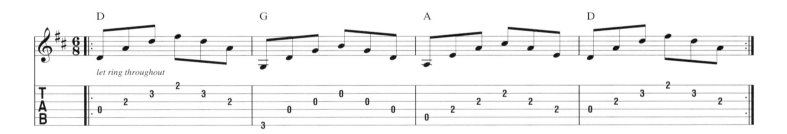

The exercise below shuffles up the order of the notes and of the fingers as it extends in length from six to eight eighth notes. Keep the finger "assignments" the same: thumb on D, index finger on G, middle finger on B, and ring finger on the high E string.

Now try the same pattern as it follows the D–G–A–D progression we played earlier:

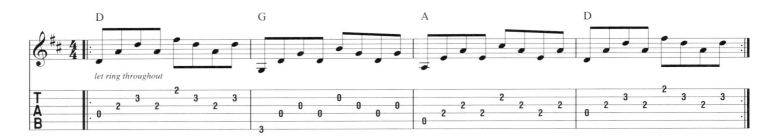

What if we want to play all the chord notes simultaneously? We can simply strum with either our thumb or index finger, using them like a pick. Each finger will sound a bit different because you will likely graze the strings with your nail if you use your index finger, resulting in a somewhat brighter tone. But there's another way to do it as well—by "grabbing" the strings with your right-hand fingers. They'll still work in the same way they did above, with the thumb moving down and the other fingers moving inwards, but they'll all be moving at the same time.

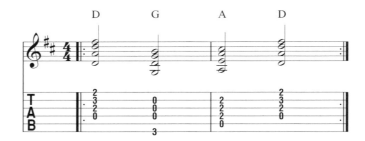

Once again, the A string was omitted from the G chord. If you wanted to include that string, simply pull upwards slightly with your grabbing fingers (particularly with the index finger), and you'll hit the B note on the A string in the process.

One of the nice things about the grabbing technique is the way you can get the best of both picking and fingerstyle techniques. In the exercise below, the thumb strikes the chord roots twice before the index, middle, and ring fingers grab the upper parts of the chord. It's a common enough groove, and most will have played something similar with a pick, but the grabbing technique allows for superior control of individual strings. You can even experiment with altering the volume of each string to emphasize certain notes once you get the hang of it.

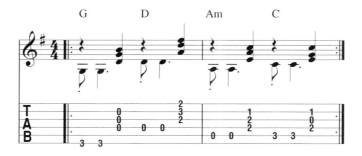

Here's a similar exercise, taken from the chorus of "You've Got a Friend." In the first measure, alternate between the thumb-plucked A roots and the grabbed notes on the D, G, and B strings, while in the second measure, they're all played at the same time.

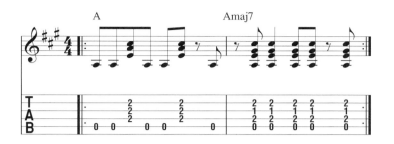

As you can see, it's a pretty cool and useful technique. Grabbing is favored by many jazz guitarists, who often strive to emulate pianists by playing each chord note simultaneously rather than strumming, which is a very "guitaristic" sound and approach.

Let's move on to a crucial technique that dominates much of the music in these pages: *Travis picking.* Named after the pioneering guitarist, singer, and songwriter Merle Travis, this technique can be quite complex but certainly needn't be in the initial stages. Guitarists of all levels can learn this style and put it to use immediately—you'll have to soon enough if you're going to play through the songs to come! The basic premise is that the thumb plays alternating bass notes that move between two strings, with the higher note usually a 5th or 3rd above the root, usually in a quarter note rhythm. (Occasionally, the root note will be alternated with one a 4th below, as in the following example.) The index and middle fingers play notes on the strings above, often in the spaces between the quarter notes or at the same time in a "pinch"-like motion. Let's begin by just using the thumb to pluck the open D and A strings. Put your left-hand fingers into a D chord shape but don't play the G, B, or high E strings.

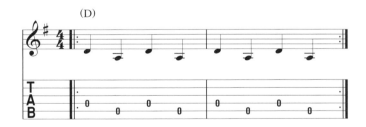

That should be easy enough, so let's add the other fingers. The thumb sticks with its D–A–D–A pattern while the middle finger plucks the high E string on beats 1 and 3 of each measure. On beats 2 and 4, the B and G strings are played in an eighth note rhythm by the middle and index fingers. Note that we have now gotten away from using the right-hand ring finger the way we did in the earliest exercises. This finger may return in more complex Travis patterns, but it's more the exception than the rule.

Next is a typical Travis pattern taken from the opening of Fleetwood Mac's "Landslide." Although the band uses a capo on the 3rd fret during the song, we will simply play the pattern over a basic C chord. In this brief excerpt, the thumb plays the A and D strings and is shown downstemmed in the notation. The index finger should play the G string notes, and the middle finger should take the notes on the B string (the notes played by these fingers are upstemmed in the notation). At the end of each measure, the thumb strikes the D string as the left-hand middle finger pulls off from the 2nd fret to the open string.

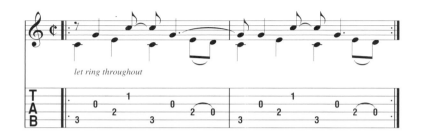

Finally, let's take a look at the opening measure of Kansas's "Dust in the Wind"—a classic example of Travis picking in action. As in the previous exercise, the thumb simply moves back and forth between C on the A string and E on the D string (the root and 3rd of the chord) in a quarter note rhythm. The middle finger plucks the B string throughout, coinciding with the thumb-plucked roots on beat 1 and falling just after the root on beat 3 of each measure. The index finger sticks strictly to the G string.

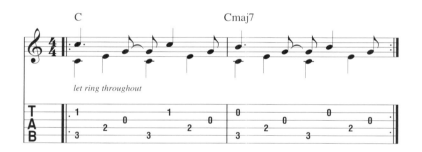

The Travis style may take some getting used to, and it's imperative that you work slowly and very carefully as you get comfortable with it. There's no sense rushing when a measured and steady pace will ensure you're doing everything right. Play the exercises above, particularly the last two, many times over until your mind and fingers have the patterns memorized and they've become second nature. Travis picking pops up repeatedly in the songs to come, so you'll have ample opportunity to put these skills to use.

There are many other fingerpicking approaches that we haven't broached—such as the rapidly vanishing Carter-style, in which the melody is played on the lower strings with chordal accompaniment played above—to cite just one. However, this chapter serves as simply an introduction to pickless playing. Once you've gotten a handle on all the songs that follow, expand your studies to include different techniques and musical genres not covered here. Perhaps you will innovate a style of your own. Your imagination and resourcefulness are the only limits.

Equipment

Most of the songs in this book were recorded on flat-top, steel-string acoustic guitars, but fingerpicking is a technique that can be used on *any* guitar. It's not a style but an approach and thus is suitable for nearly any genre. You can and should try all of the songs that follow on any guitar you have handy, if only to experience the different technical demands of playing this way on an electric guitar, nylon string, and so on. Electric guitars provide solo overdubs on John Mayer's "The Heart of Life" and Fleetwood Mac's "Landslide." Nylon-string guitars are used on Eric Clapton's "Tears in Heaven" and Mason William's "Classical Gas." As you switch guitars, you may notice that barre chords are harder to play on a nylon-string guitar, which will usually have a flat (or even a slightly convex) fretboard radius. Conversely, they will likely be easier on an electric, as most (but not all) techniques are. The wider span of a nylon-string neck may be somewhat more difficult to negotiate for players with smaller hands. On the flip side, those with big fingers may find it's easier to get all the strings ringing and each note in a chord sounding clearly with the noticeably wider spacing. Beginners with tender fingertips may also find the nylon strings easier to press and hold down, although all players must eventually develop the strength and calluses required to eliminate this concern entirely.

One of the pleasures of acoustic fingerpicking is the simplicity of the sound and of selecting equipment. Get yourself a good guitar that stays in tune, isn't too hard to play, and has consistent intonation up and down the neck. That's pretty much it. If you are a performing or recording artist, the matter is complicated somewhat by the need for amplification. There are numerous choices on the market today in terms of after-market pickups that can be affixed to an acoustic guitar without screws or drilling. If you expect to require amplification on a consistent basis, most manufacturers also offer both steel and nylon string acoustic guitars that come with on-board pickups, equalization, and even digital tuners—a tremendous convenience to be sure. Remember as always that you get what you pay for, and a very inexpensive guitar with all these features is unlikely to be of professional quality. Play any prospective purchases both amplified and unplugged (the tone should be strong and attractive without the use of electronics) and test it at room and performance volumes if at all possible. Some amplified acoustics have a tendency to buzz or especially to feed back at higher volumes. The better offerings will usually minimize these tendencies.

Depending on your personal requirements, you may need no amp at all, a small amp designed expressly for acoustic guitars, or even a complete PA system with microphones, monitors, and the like. Take your time and carefully consider where and what you'll be playing before spending your hard-earned money. Many is the overzealous guitarist who maxes out their credit cards on gear before realizing that most of it will never even leave the house and see the light of day. Additionally, the acoustic guitar market has in recent years become inundated with the work of numerous independent luthiers, who craft a very small number of instruments a year. These guitars can be extremely beautiful and expressive but are often very expensive when compared to those made by the bigger corporate builders. If you can afford such an instrument, then have at it—they are playable works of art and may become your lifelong companion. Just take your time playing a wide range of guitars and be a discerning comparison shopper. A top shelf acoustic can easily run into a high four figure price tag.

One piece of gear that will be helpful in playing some of the music to come is a *capo*—a type of clamping device that spans the fretboard, thus shortening it and allowing you to play traditional, open-string chord shapes such as G, D, E minor, and the like in higher keys without changing your fingering. Today's capos are vastly improved over the old models that required you to fasten them in place awkwardly and tended to dampen strings and mess with pitch accuracy. A company like Dunlop makes a variety of steel capos with protective rubber padding that stay put, pop on and off with a simple squeeze, and won't damage your strings or your guitar's neck in any way. Most of them retail at under twenty dollars, so you won't be making much of an investment in something that should last for decades. You can, of course, play any of the capoed songs without this device, but you will have to move down the neck into the keys of A minor ("Scarborough Fair/Canticle"), C ("Landslide" and "Don't Think Twice, It's All Right"), and G ("You've Got a Friend"), and you won't be able to play along with the original recordings (unless you're a fan of seriously dissonant sounds).

Scarborough Fair/Canticle

By Simon & Garfunkel
From *Parsley, Sage, Rosemary and Thyme* (1996)

Arrangement and Original Counter Melody by
Paul Simon and Arthur Garfunkel

Copyright © 1966 (Renewed) Paul Simon and Arthur Garfunkel (BMI)
International Copyright Secured   All Rights Reserved
Used by Permission

Standard tuning pitches

TRACK 01

Simon and Garfunkel's interpretation of this old English folk song has a wonderfully mysterious air and a sense of the baroque—qualities that have helped to make it one of the duo's best loved and most enduring recordings. The purity of both their voices and of the simple, evocative chords transport the listener to an era far removed from the technology-crazed, warp-speed contemporary world. It's a fitting place to begin our exploration of fingerstyle guitar, an art which in and of itself stands as a reminder of simpler days—an era of a musician and a guitar, using their hands to craft a simple, beautiful song. The only technology you'll need here is a capo affixed to your instrument's 7th fret. This relatively high capo position accommodates the singers' vocal range but also lends the guitar a uniquely harp-like effect. The tab indicates the frets to be played relative to the capo position (the capoed fret is "0"), while the standard notation and chords simply sound a perfect 5th higher than indicated.

Introduction

This section is played on five strings (A through high E), but Paul Simon employs just four right-hand fingers; the pinky of the picking hand, as mentioned in the earlier lesson chapter, is almost never used. The thumb should pluck all the notes on the A and D strings, while the ring finger plays the high E string notes, the middle finger plays the B string, and the index finger plucks the G string. In the left hand, the 1st and 2nd fingers should be used to play the B and D string notes in measures 1, 2, 4, and 6. The 1st finger should also play both A string notes in measure 3.

TRACK 02

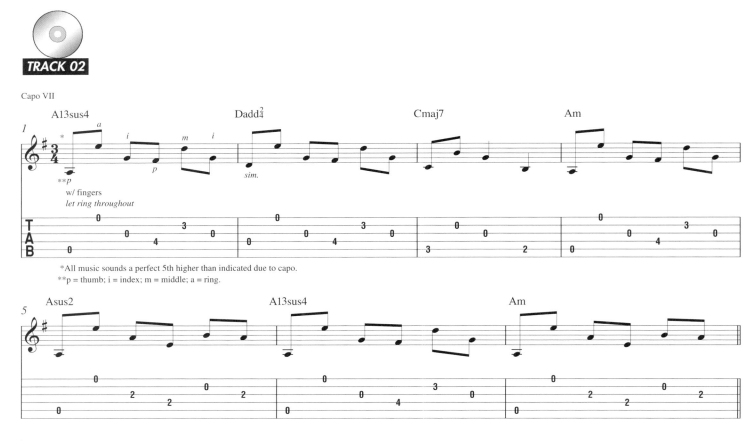

Verse (Part I)

This section marks the entrance of the vocals and features the same A chord shapes encountered in the introduction. The picking stays close to the template set in the intro, but there are a few minor alterations. For the G chord in measure 3, pluck the low E and B strings simultaneously with your thumb and ring finger, then follow by plucking the open G and D strings with your middle and index fingers as they close inwards towards your palm. In measures 6 and 7, two of your left-hand fingers can remain in place, with your 2nd finger on the D string and your 1st finger on the B string above. For the D chord in measure 8, your thumb should pluck the D string while your index, middle, and ring fingers pluck the G, B, and high E strings, respectively.

TRACK 03

Verse (Part II)

The 12 measures below complete the song form; combine them with the previous example and repeat the entire 24-measure progression for each new verse. At the end of measure 1 below, use three consecutive thumb stokes on the A string to rise from the open string to the 3rd fret (C), which begins measure 2. Your left hand should remain in position throughout the first 5 measures, so that your 3rd finger plays all 3rd fret notes, your 2nd finger takes all 2nd fret notes, and your 1st finger plays each C on the B string's 1st fret. There's a somewhat tricky maneuver in measure 8 in which you perform a hammer-on and pull-off with your 2nd and 1st fingers on the D and B strings simultaneously. After plucking the open strings, be sure to come down with enough force to sound the E and C combination, then pull *down* slightly as you lift off to re-sound the open strings. The example concludes with a return to the droning Asus voicings encountered in the two previous excerpts.

TRACK 04

Landslide

By Fleetwood Mac
From *Fleetwood Mac* (1975)

Words and Music by Stevie Nicks

Copyright © 1975 Welsh Witch Music
Copyright Renewed
All Rights Administered by Sony/ATV Music Publishing LLC, 8 Music Square West, Nashville, TN 37203
International Copyright Secured   All Rights Reserved

This gentle, extremely popular ballad is a confirmed fingerpicking classic. Although it is closely associated with its composer, the charismatic Stevie Nicks, and was famously covered by the Dixie Chicks, it appeals to both men and women alike and is a staple in the repertoire of countless acoustic guitarists. It's easy to sing too, although men may want to play it without a capo (dropping the key from E♭ to C) to accommodate a lower vocal range.

Intro and Verse Accompaniment

"Landslide" is a quintessential Travis picking song. It could be approached in a few different ways in terms of right-hand technique, but the Travis style is by far the most sensible. For the central riff shown below, your thumb will play the A and D string notes while alternating with your index and middle fingers, which should take care of the notes on the G and B strings above. Play through the passage slowly and carefully, staying strictly with this picking arrangement, until it becomes second nature. The left-hand maneuvers are fairly simple. Begin with a standard open C shape and pull off with your 2nd finger to the open D string at the end of beat 4. The D on the B string's 3rd fret in the G/B chords should be played with the 4th finger while your 2nd finger takes care of the B note on the A string below. Notice how the final note of the example, the open B string, rings on as you begin the repeat, creating a particularly lovely resonance. Be sure to arch your left-hand fingers sufficiently throughout the song to allow all the strings to ring as long as possible. If you flatten out and choke the notes off, the song will quickly lose the luster that makes it so appealing.

TRACK 05

*All music sounds a minor 3rd higher than indicated due to capo.

Verse Extension

This nicely layered section bridges the gap between the song's second verse and the initial chorus. The two guitars, which have been playing in unison up to this point, now split apart into separate parts that are similar but different enough to create a richer harmonic and textural feeling. Learn each part and, if possible, team up with a friend to hear the way they intertwine and complement each other. Guitar 1 begins very much like the main verse riff pattern but quickly increases in intricacy, so approach this part with care. As stated earlier, the more you can discipline yourself to maintaining strict picking patterns, the faster you will master the technique as a whole and create a solid technical base for future playing. Remember that the faster and more challenging the music, the more it becomes absolutely essential that your picking technique is sound and organized. Lecture over, for now; let's talk specifics.

Measure 1 follows the pattern of the previous example. In measure 3, reach out to grab the high G with your *ring* finger, then resume the alternating picking pattern, plucking the D string with your thumb and hammering on from the open string to the 2nd fret with your 2nd finger. To play the G/B figure in measure 4, pluck the A and high E strings simultaneously with your thumb and ring finger, the G string with your index finger, then the D and B string grouping with your thumb and middle finger, finishing by plucking the high E string again with your ring finger. The remainder of the measure returns to the initial Travis picking configuration. It's an intricate little piece of work, so take your time bringing it up to speed. In measure 6, approach the same chord in a similar fashion, with the D notes on the B string picked by the middle finger while your thumb picks the A and D string notes and your middle finger picks the G string notes below. Use the same arrangement in measure 4, with your middle finger picking all B string notes and your thumb moving down to the low E string to pluck the root of the D7/F♯ chord.

Now let's turn our attention to the part played by Guitar 2, which is even more detailed. Any notes that occur on the high E string should be picked by the ring finger, allowing the thumb, index, and middle fingers to remain as close to the original Travis pattern as possible. Be very meticulous in plotting your fingering here. If you stray from the pattern too far, ask yourself if you will really be able to pull off your "altered" picking arrangement at full speed–things that seem easy at practice tempo are often nearly impossible when the speed is cranked up. Finally, the 16th note pull-off and hammer-on figure in measure 7 should be played with your left-hand 2nd finger doing all the work on both D and G strings.

TRACK 06

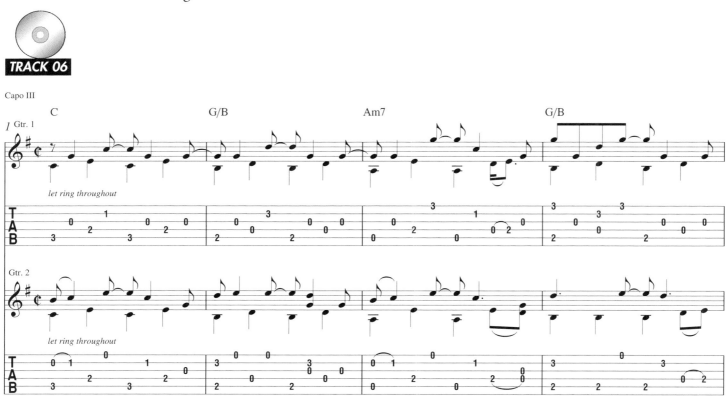

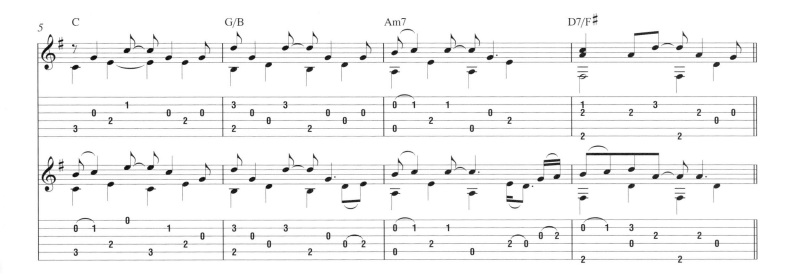

Chorus

This 16-measure section also features twin guitars layered on top of each other to form a richly textured arrangement. Once more, we will examine each part separately, beginning with Guitar 1. Start by adhering to the initial Travis picking pattern, but bring the ring finger into the mix as required for the many high E string notes. During the D7/F# chord, your thumb should pluck the low E and D strings while your index and middle fingers pick the G and B strings, respectively.

Guitar 2 has a slightly simpler part this time in that it adheres more closely to the original Travis pattern. The first measure should be picked as follows: thumb on the low E string, plucking simultaneously with the middle finger on the B string, followed by the thumb picking the open D string. In measure 2, the thumb should be assigned to the low E and D strings while the index finger grabs the G string notes. In measure 4, the thumb will pick the E, A, and D strings. Shuffling the picking up incorrectly will make a mess of the whole passage, so study the part carefully and take note of the more challenging spots to preempt any picking issues from cropping up.

TRACK 07

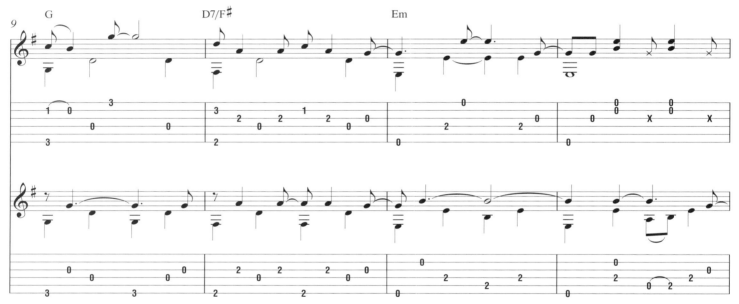

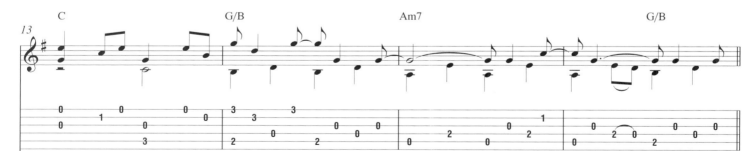

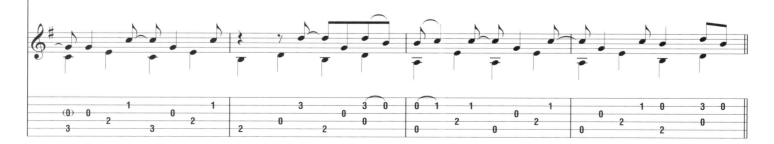

Blackbird

By the Beatles
From _The Beatles (the White Album)_ (1968)

Words and Music by
John Lennon and Paul McCartney

Copyright © 1968, 1969 Sony/ATV Music Publishing LLC
Copyright Renewed
All Rights Administered by Sony/ATV Music Publishing LLC, 8 Music Square West, Nashville, TN 37203
International Copyright Secured   All Rights Reserved

This charming little Beatles chestnut is amongst the most widely played fingerstyle songs in existence and is doubtless one of the most requested of guitar teachers by students around the world. It's easy to see why: it has a delicate feeling and sound on the instrument, it combines harmonic richness with a bluesy sensibility, and it has a highly singable, memorable vocal melody of the type that seemed to flow from these songwriters like water from a spigot. It also sounds a good deal more complex than it actually is, but there are a number of challenges to be faced here, not least of which are the shifting time signatures that require careful counting as the song unfolds.

Verse

"Blackbird" is comprised of only two distinct sections: the 10-measure verse below and the five-measure bridge that follows. As you examine the music, you will see there are numerous instances in which two strings are played simultaneously in a variety of ways. In the opening measure, the low E or A string is paired with a higher note on the B string while alternating with the open G string. In measure 2, the G and B strings are struck together repeatedly. Many people will play this song with three right-hand fingers—namely the thumb, index, and middle fingers—but Paul McCartney used just his thumb and index finger to play the entire song. Each time notes are played on two *non-consecutive* strings at the same time, use your thumb and index finger on the low and high notes, respectively. In the case of two-note groupings on *consecutive* strings, use your index finger to lightly strum them both down and up (this also applies to the three-note grouping in measure 8).

Left-hand fingering will require a small amount of consideration as well. Begin the song with your 3rd finger taking the G on the low E string, then play the G/B chord with your 1st finger on the A string and your 4th finger on the B string. This will allow you to slide up the neck and spread your fingers apart as you play the G chord in measure 2. The picking in this measure (and in subsequent rhythmically similar spots) should be as follows: Pluck the 5th and 2nd strings simultaneously with the thumb and index finger, then strum the next two two-note groupings with the index finger, going down and then up. Follow by plucking the A string with your thumb, picking the G string with an index finger upstroke, then strumming the G and B strings with an index finger downstroke. The entire process is repeated a second time within the measure.

In measures 3 and 5, the C and D chords should be played with your left-hand 1st finger on the A string and 4th finger on the B string, while the C♯° and D♯° chords should be played by your 2nd and 1st fingers on the A and high E strings, respectively. Follow this type of fingering scheme throughout the song, and you'll be in good shape. Return to the right-hand approach outlined for measure 2 above each time you encounter a similar rhythmic figure, such as in measures 6 and 7 (although you will essentially use the same picking pattern, with subtle variations, in measures 8 through 10 as well).

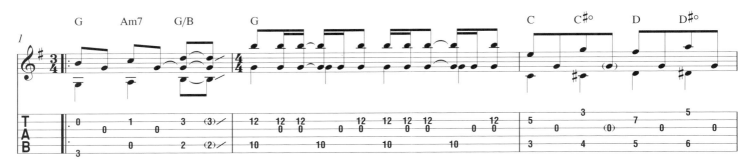

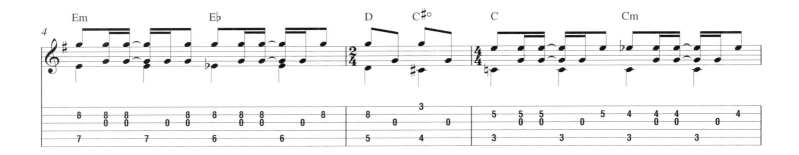

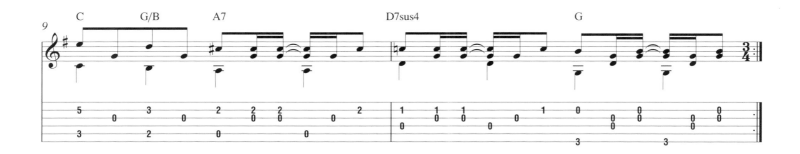

Chorus

This five-measure section shouldn't present too many problems if you've already mastered the verse riffs above; all the techniques discussed there apply here as well. The picking is exactly the same, alternating between thumb and index finger groupings and index finger strummed notes on the G and B strings. As far as the left hand is concerned, the 1st finger should play all A string notes, walking up and down the string as indicated. You can play all the B string notes leading up to the A7 chord with your 4th finger as Paul does, or you may alternate between your 4th and 3rd fingers depending on whether the note in question is one or two frets above the A string note played at the same time. The choice is yours; either way has its upsides and drawbacks. During the final measure, in a 2/4 time signature, the F on the high E string is lightly grazed, making it more of an implied than an explicitly stated pitch. Don't agonize over it! Leave it out entirely or keep it in as you like; just don't emphasize it unnecessarily. And have fun—this song is truly a classic.

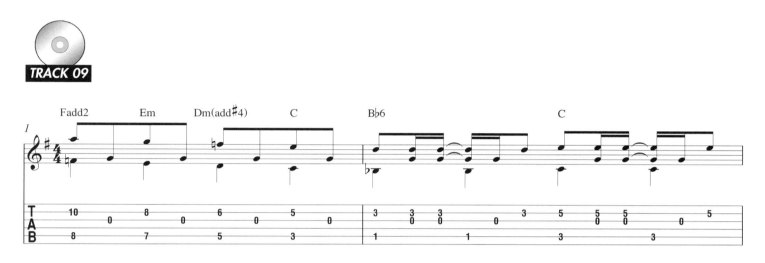

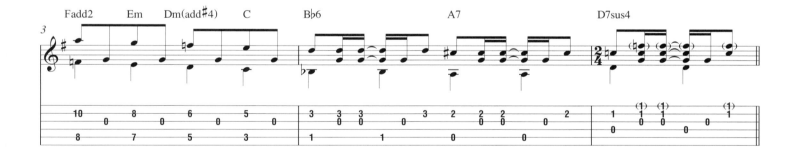

Dust in the Wind

By Kansas
From *Point of Know Return* (1977)

Words and Music by Kerry Livgren

© 1977 (Renewed 2005), 1978 EMI BLACKWOOD MUSIC INC. and DON KIRSHNER MUSIC
All Rights Controlled and Administered by EMI BLACKWOOD MUSIC INC.
All Rights Reserved   International Copyright Secured   Used by Permission

While many guitar fans would think first of "Carry on Wayward Son" when prog-rock supergroup Kansas is mentioned, "Dust in the Wind" was perhaps the band's biggest hit. This pensive acoustic number is a perfect fingerpicking vehicle and a great song to whip out for a solo performance—particularly if you are a somewhat competent vocalist to boot. The various open position chord shapes played by the left hand should be easy enough for even beginning players to learn quickly, allowing the guitarist to concentrate on developing their fingerpicking skills in earnest.

Intro

"Dust in the Wind" is another Travis picking–based song, and strict adherence to that approach will serve you well here. As with all new material, go through each section slowly and carefully, with as many repetitions as are needed to get yourself used to the very specific right-hand finger-to-string "assignments" and to build up both speed and the muscle memory necessary to pull the song off at full tempo.

Let's get to the specifics. Luckily, the picking scheme employed in the intro will carry through the bulk of the song, so once you get a hang of it, you will be in good shape. Your thumb should pluck all notes on the A and D strings below, while your middle finger will pick the B string (often simultaneously with the A string), and your index finger will take the notes on the G string. That's it! Stick to that arrangement without variation, and you'll be golden. As far as the left hand is concerned, you will be holding down basic C and Am open position chord shapes while performing subtle maneuvers that do not require much hand movement at all. For the C shapes, simply lift your 1st finger from the B string for Cmaj7 and use your 4th finger on the same string, at the 3rd fret, for each Cadd9 chord. As you transition to the various Am chords, your 2nd finger should remain stationary on the D string, while your 1st and 4th fingers perform the same moves on the B string to create the Am and Amsus4 chords. Keep your fingers well arched to allow all the strings in each chord to ring as freely as possible, generating a rich, full, and resonant sound as your guitar really begins to vibrate and sing.

TRACK 10

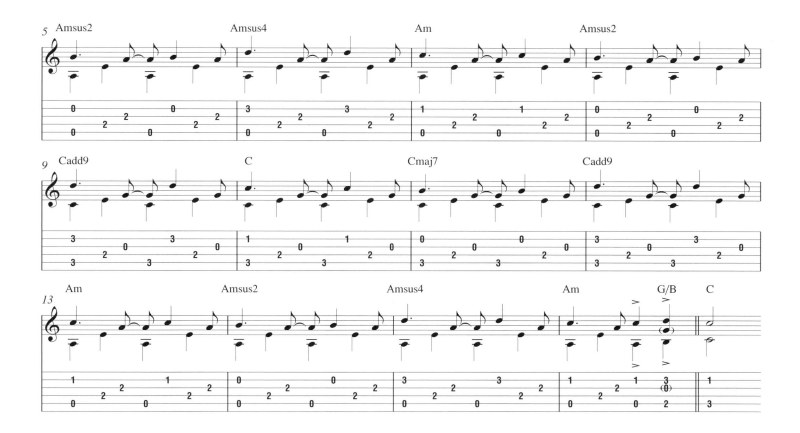

Verse

Before discussing the right-hand duties in this section, let's take a moment to examine the fingerings of the various chord shapes played by the left hand. The C, G/B (G in first inversion, with the 3rd of the chord in the bass), and Am chords that begin the excerpt should pose no questions. In measures 5 and 6, play the root of the G with your 2nd finger, then the Dm7 chord with your 3rd, 1st, and 2nd fingers on the G, B, and high E strings, respectively. Perform the pull-off at the end of the measure with your 3rd finger lifting off to sound the open G string. The D/F# chord (again, a first inversion of a major chord with the 3rd in the bass) in measures 17 and 21 should be played with the 1st finger on the low E string and the 2nd and 3rd fingers on the G and B strings. In measures 19 and 20, stay in the standard Am fingering and simply add your 4th finger to the low E string's 3rd fret as you transition to the Am/G chord.

The picking in this section follows the same pattern established in the intro as much as possible, with the two-note groupings plucked by the thumb and middle fingers. In true Travis fashion, the thumb will pluck the lowest two notes of each chord throughout the example. Additionally, the middle finger should grab all notes on the B and high E strings. The thumb will have to do a little string skipping here as well, as it jumps from the low E string to the D string and back in measures 5, 13, 17, 18, 20, 21, and 22 for the G, Am/G, and D/F# chords.

TRACK 11

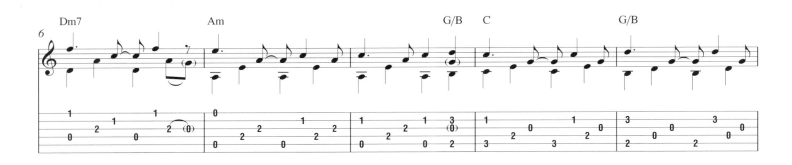

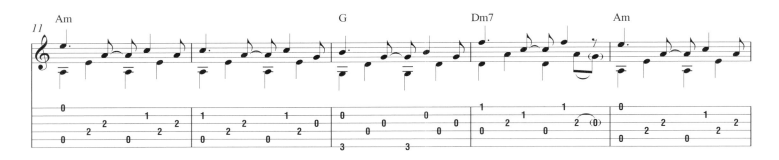

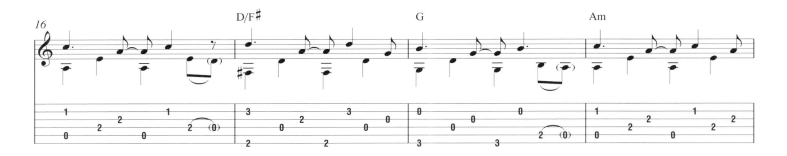

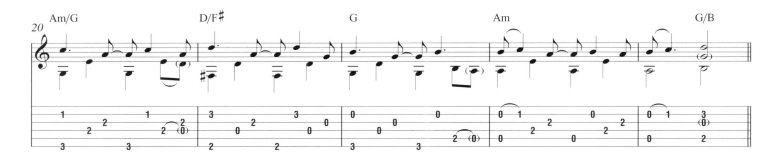

Violin Solo Accompaniment

This short riff is repeated under the violin solo played by Robbie Steinhardt. The picking pattern is identical to the earlier sections. In the left hand, the 3rd and 1st fingers take the A and C on the D and G strings, respectively, during the Am(add2) chord, while the 1st and *4th* fingers should play the D and G string notes during the F(#11)/A. This will allow you to grab the D on the B string's 3rd fret with your 2nd finger for the F6(#11)/A chord in measure 7.

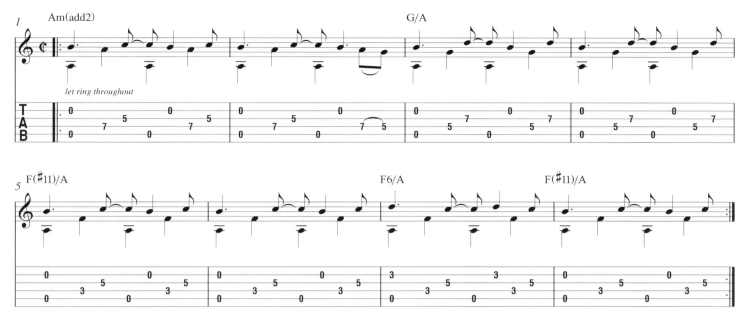

Outro

This repeat-and-fade riff is a little trickier than it initially seems. The picking retains the same basic pattern as the other parts of the song, but the index finger may be omitted entirely. Instead, the middle finger can pick all the B and high E string notes while the thumb takes care of the A and D string (the G string isn't used at all). This two-fingered approach simplifies matters greatly in terms of the picking. In the left hand, the 2nd finger should remain on the D string's 2nd fret, without lifting off, throughout the phrase. The 1st finger will take the 1st fret notes on the B and high E string, while the 4th finger takes the 3rd fret D on the B string in each Amsus4(♭13) chord.

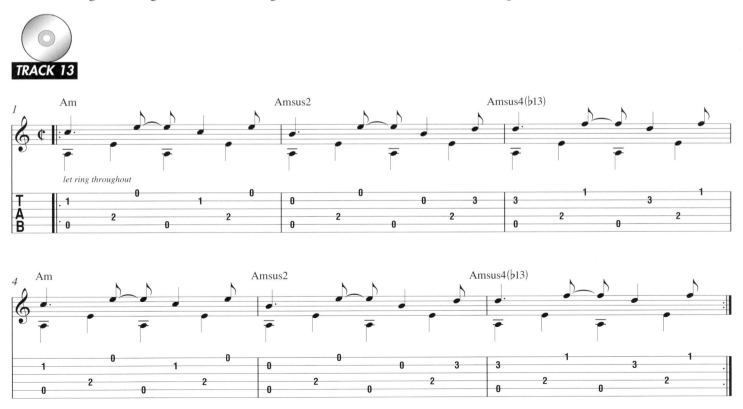

Helplessly Hoping

By Crosby, Stills & Nash
From *Crosby, Stills & Nash* (1969)

Words and Music by Stephen Stills

Copyright © 1969 Gold Hill Music, Inc.
Copyright Renewed
All Rights Reserved   Used by Permission

This gorgeous song from the iconic folk trio's debut album uses Travis picking as its template while also introducing some subtle variations that raise the bar a bit in terms of overall difficulty. It's a simple song on the surface, with basic chords that allow the harmonized vocals to come to the fore, but the details in the guitar accompaniment, while not exceedingly difficult, do merit close attention and perhaps a little extra practice time as well. After you've mastered the basic elements of the song—namely the picking patterns and left-hand chord shapes—be sure you include all the hammer-ons, index finger strums, and staccato notes indicated in the notation.

Intro

This eight-measure section moves Am7–C–G–D, all in their most common open-string fingerings. The only technical considerations for the left hand are the four hammer-ons in the phrase. Each requires you to come down with sufficient force to sound the fretted note after plucking the open string. The hammer-ons in measures 5 and 6, "inside" the G chord, are particularly challenging because your 2nd finger must sound the E on the D string's 2nd fret without being picked while the open G is picked simultaneously. It's a bit of an odd maneuver, so you'll want to practice it slowly enough to get both hands working together in the proper order before you bring the phrase back up to speed.

For the right hand, take note of the up-and-down index finger strums in measures 7 and 8; they are marked above the notation and recur throughout the tune, breaking up the more traditional finger picking patterns (the same technique was examined in our discussion of "Blackbird"). Otherwise, stick closely to the Travis pattern, with your thumb plucking all notes on the low E, A, and D strings and your index finger plucking the G string. Your middle finger should pick all the notes on both the B and high E strings.

TRACK 14

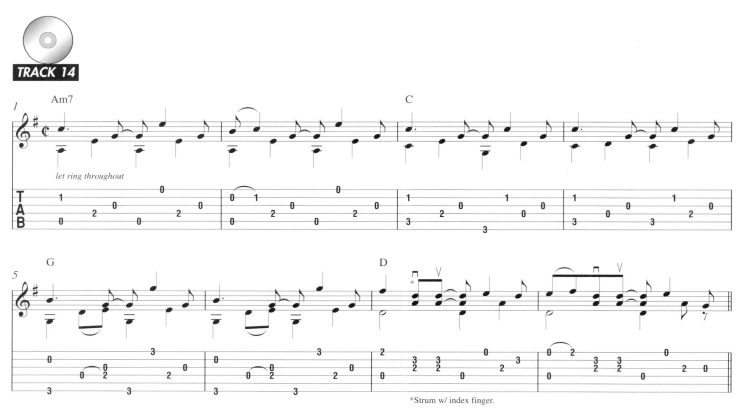

*Strum w/ index finger.

Verse

This somewhat lengthy verse has both a 1st ending leading back to the beginning of the section and a 2nd ending that takes us to the chorus. The chord sequence in the opening eight bars is basically repeated in measures 9–16, although there are plenty of right-hand variations along the way. For the most part, the same chord shapes from the intro appear here as well, although the final G7sus4 chord is new. Play this one with your 3rd finger on the low E string and your 1st finger barring the B and high E strings at the 1st fret. You may also play any G chords with your left-hand thumb taking the roots on the low E string's 3rd fret (as described in the chorus section). Take note of the various index finger strums in the excerpt (again, indicated by the symbols above the notation) and of the hammer-ons that pop up occasionally. There's a full chord hammer-on in measure 13 in which your 2nd and 1st fingers must come down hard enough on the D and B strings, respectively, to sound the C/G chord.

The right-hand picking patterns remain in keeping with the Travis-style techniques established earlier, with the thumb plucking the low E, A, and D strings, the index finger taking the notes on the G string, and your middle finger picking the B and high E strings. All strums should be played by the index finger regardless of what strings are being used.

TRACK 15

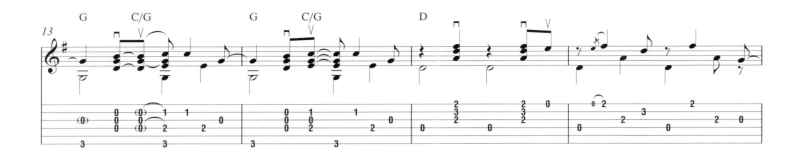

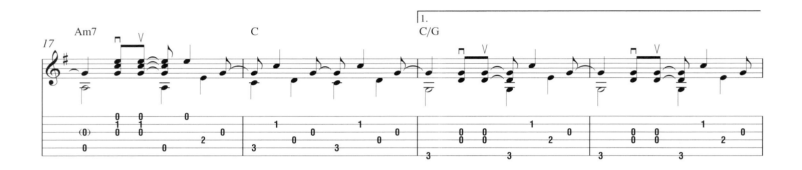

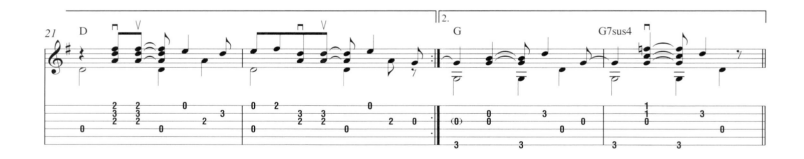

Chorus I

"Helplessly Hoping" has two distinct choruses with separate chord progressions and accompaniment patterns. In each, Stephen Stills hooks his left-hand thumb over the neck to play the G's on the low E string's 3rd fret. If this technique is new to you, give it a little time, and you should be able to pull it off; it can be particularly challenging for those with hands that are on the smaller side, though. During the Gsus4 chords, add your 1st finger to the B string's 1st fret and use your 3rd finger to barre the top two strings at the 3rd fret for the G5 chord. This arrangement of the left-hand fingers allows you to remain stationery throughout the excerpt, which is a great advantage and will aid in creating a resonant, freely ringing sound. The D and B string hammer-on seen in the previous example returns here in the penultimate measure. Follow with a strummed three-note C chord, then use the tip of your overhanging thumb to prevent the open A string in the final chord from ringing.

TRACK 16

Chorus II

The final chorus of the song, shown below, uses the index finger strum much more extensively to give the section a slightly forceful feel in contrast to the gentler fingerpicked passages. Once more the left-hand thumb should play the G roots, with 3rd finger barres on the 3rd fret of the B and high E strings for all G5 chords. The G7sus4 chords require you to reach back with your 1st finger and barre the same strings at the 1st fret. This fingering arrangement holds true during the final five measures, when the 3rd finger plays the root of the Fsus2 chord on the D string and the 1st finger does the 1st fret barring. The Csus2 chord is played like a conventional C chord, minus the 2nd finger on the D string (although it does hammer-on to its usual spot in measure 10). The song ends with the D and B string dual hammer-ons encountered earlier. The 3rd finger plays the final note on the high E string.

Don't Think Twice, It's All Right

By Bob Dylan
From *The Freewheelin' Bob Dylan* (1963)

Words and Music by Bob Dylan

Copyright © 1963 Warner Bros. Inc.
Copyright Renewed 1991 Special Rider Music
International Copyright Secured   All Rights Reserved
Reprinted by Permission of Music Sales Corporation

On this enduring early offering from the sly, sardonic master folk songwriter, Dylan exhibits impressively fluid Travis picking skills. Although the song has a casual, breezy feel, the guitar parts move by pretty quickly, so slow everything way down and practice the constituent parts for as long as you need to before ratcheting the speed back up to the full tempo. Dylan uses a capo at the 4th fret on the original recording to raise the sounded key from C to E; the notation and chords above (as well as the analysis) represent the shapes played relative to the capo placement (the capoed fret is "0" in the tab).

Intro

In this section and the verse excerpts that follow, examine the left-hand chord voicings and be sure you have them under your fingers before applying the Travis pattern played by the right hand. All the G chord shapes should be played with your 3rd finger on the low E string. For the Am7/G chord, the 4th finger should play the low G in the same place (3rd fret of the low E string), allowing your other fingers to stay in place on what is essentially an open position Am chord raised to C♯m by the capo.

By now, the basics of Travis picking should be getting pretty familiar. In this song, the thumb will pluck the bottom two strings of each chord, the index finger will play the G string notes, and the middle finger will pluck the B and high E strings. Notes on the B and high E strings often coincide with one on the low E string in a two-note combination "pinch." In measure 3, for instance, the right-hand fingering would be: thumb, index, thumb, thumb, index, thumb, middle finger. Measure 4 begins with the thumb plucking the low E string while your left-hand 1st finger hammers on to the B string (your left-hand thumb should hook over the top of neck to play the root of the F chord). Follow with the index, thumb, and middle fingers and then finish with the thumb, index, thumb, and middle finger.

On paper it sounds more complex than it really is, although it's certainly not what you'd call "easy"—at least not at first. Take your time carefully building your Travis chops and you'll get back what you put into it. As I wrote earlier, it's worth agonizing somewhat over the minute details of this style and being very disciplined in the way that you apply it, as your diligence in the early stages will pay off with greatly increased speed and ease of execution in the long run.

TRACK 18

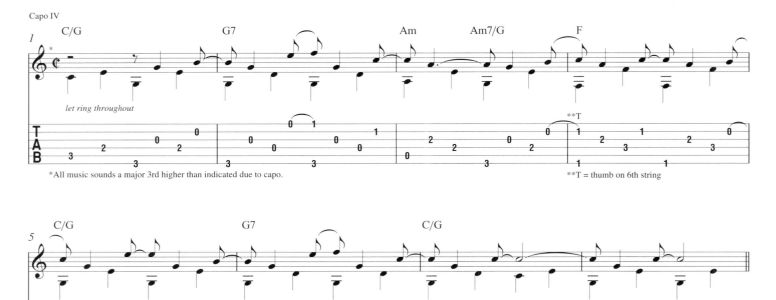

*All music sounds a major 3rd higher than indicated due to capo.

**T = thumb on 6th string

Verse (Part I)

This 16-measure excerpt includes all of the chords from the intro, although the rate at which they change has been altered somewhat. This shift in the "harmonic rhythm" really helps to make the song that much more interesting and unpredictable. There's also the introduction of a new chord, D7/F♯, in measures 13–14, which is the II7 chord in first inversion (the 3rd, F♯, is the lowest note, rather than the D). The left-hand 2nd finger should play the F♯ on the low E string, while your 3rd and 1st fingers get to the notes on the G and B strings, respectively. The picking in these two measures will use the thumb, index, and middle fingers as established earlier, with two consecutive thumb strokes between the 3rd and 4th notes in each measure.

There are numerous instances in this song in which a hammer-on along the high E or B string coincides with a plucked note on the low E string, which is a tricky move to pull off at first but one that becomes increasingly intuitive (much like the Travis picking technique in general). Avoid "pinching" the two strings with the thumb and middle finger in these instances, although it may seem like the easiest approach at the outset. Instead, work on your timing with both hands *and* both strings in question. We saw this technique at work in "Helplessly Hoping;" it features prominently here, so be patient and put your practice time in until you get over the hump.

Capo IV

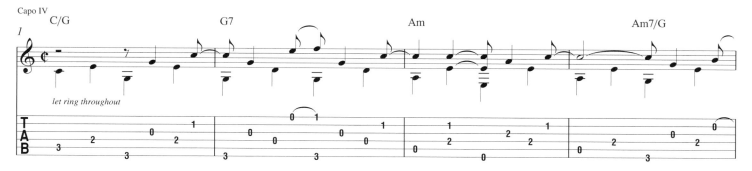

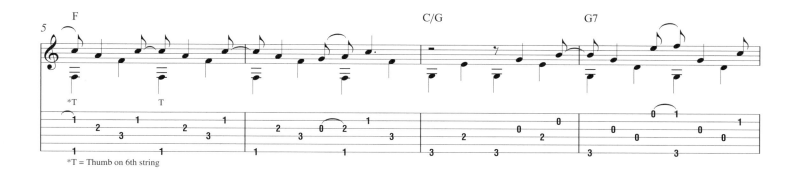

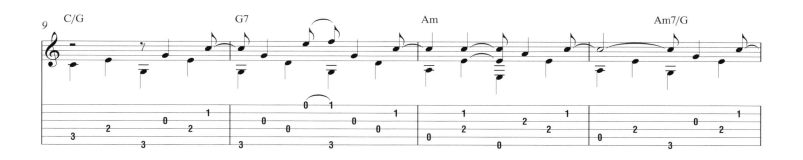

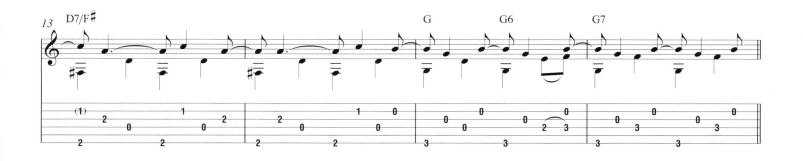

Verse (Part II)

The second half of the song form begins below, in another 16-measure excerpt. The only new chord in this example is the C7 chord formed by adding the 4th finger to the G string's 3rd fret while the 1st finger in the C/G shape stays in place and the 3rd finger crosses strings from the low E to the A. This segment of the song should prove to be the easiest yet if you've worked your way through the earlier parts carefully, as the picking patterns here are very repetitive and stick to the basic Travis style very closely. The thumb should play all the low E, A, and D notes, while the index finger sticks to the G string, and the middle finger grabs the B and high E strings on top. Follow this formula without alteration, and you'll breeze right through.

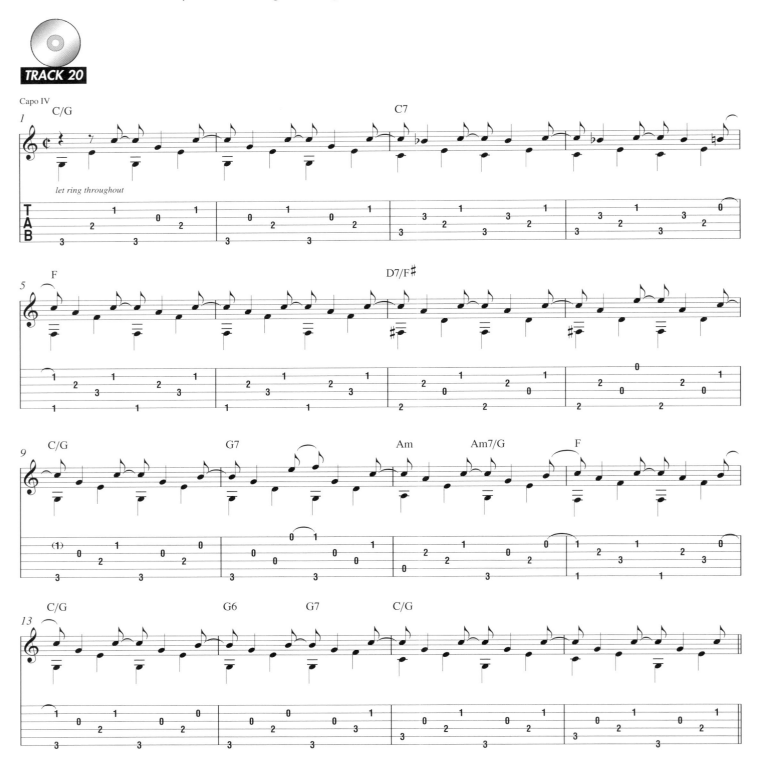

You've Got a Friend

By James Taylor
From *Mud Slide Slim and the Blue Horizon* (1971)

Words and Music by Carole King

© 1971 (Renewed 1999) COLGEMS-EMI MUSIC INC.
All Rights Reserved   International Copyright Secured   Used by Permission

One of a string of early hits that helped propel James Taylor to stardom, "You've Got a Friend," written by singer/songwriter Carole King, is one of those tunes that everyone knows and loves to sing along to. It unfolds with a sense of inevitability but has layers of complexity that may go unnoticed by the casual listener. The guitar part is intricate and carefully picked, with a great degree of finesse and delicacy. Taylor, singing the lead and playing (with a capo affixed to the 2nd fret) won a Grammy award for his performance of this song, and it's easy to see why; it's beautiful and timeless, melodic and uplifting.

Intro

Throughout this song, Taylor's capoed guitar is notated in G but sounds a major 2nd higher (in the key of A) due to the capo. The chord symbols are also written in G. James uses four right hand fingers to pick the strings, getting a bit away from the Travis-picking style of the previous songs in this book. In the intro below, the thumb will play the low E and A string notes, while the index, middle, and ring fingers will take the G, B, and high E strings, respectively. The open D string in measure 2 should be played by the thumb as well. In the final measure, the string assignments shift down a string, so the index finger takes the D string, the middle finger takes the G string, and the ring finger plucks the B string.

With regards to the left hand, be sure to use your 3rd finger for the 3rd fret roots on the C and G chords. The 4th finger will play the G notes on the high E string's 3rd fret. In measure 4, the 1st finger should play the roots of each chord on the low E and A strings.

TRACK 21

*All music sounds a major 2nd higher than indicated due to capo.

Verse (Part I)

This eight-measure section allows the left hand to remain fairly stationary in 1st position (relative to the capo), with little in the way of lateral movement. The right-hand thumb should pluck all of the low E and A string notes as well as the open D string roots of the D7sus4 chord in measure 6. In measure 2, the left-hand 2nd finger should move back and forth between the B and F♯ on the 2nd fret of the lower two strings while the 1st and 3rd fingers remain in place on the D and G strings above. The 2nd finger will remain in place on the A string's 2nd fret in the following measure before moving up to the 2nd fret of the D string in measures 4 and 5 and the 2nd fret of the G string in measure 6. In the final two measures, the picking on the top three strings should be assigned strictly to the index, middle, and ring fingers.

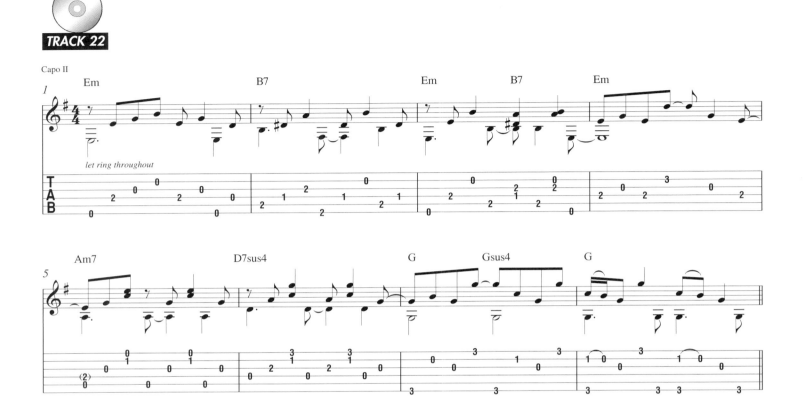

Verse (Part II)

The excerpt below extends the verse and leads the song beautifully into the chorus. In the opening measure, Taylor uses his 1st finger to barre the strings at the 2nd fret while the right-hand thumb plucks the low E and A strings and the D, G, and B strings are assigned to the index, middle, and ring fingers, respectively. In measure 2, the same three fingers "grab" the strings for the three-note B7 and B7sus4 groupings. Measures 3–5 are played in 1st position, with the left-hand 1st finger taking the C on the B string during the Am7 chord. In the final two measures, the 4th finger should play the 3rd fret high E string notes and pull off to the 3rd finger at the end of the example.

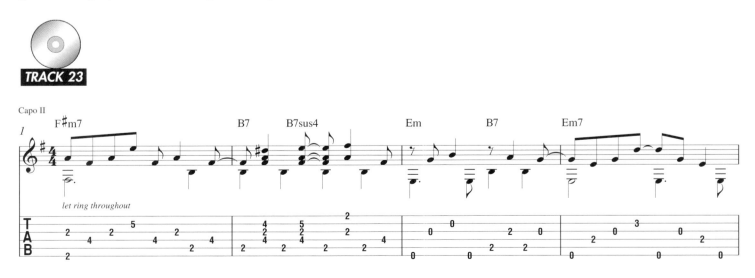

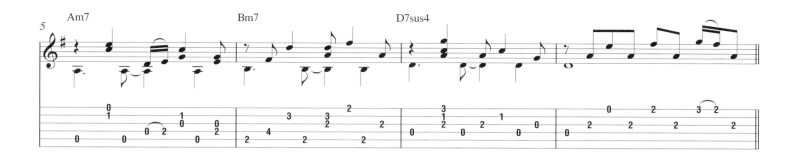

Chorus

The chorus of this song is basically a 16-measure section with a two-measure extension growing organically out of the melodic figure played by the guitars in measures 15 and 16. Begin the example with your 3rd finger playing the chord roots on the low E and A strings. Pluck these notes with your thumb and use your index, middle, and ring fingers to play the notes on the G, B, and high E strings, respectively. Remember to grab and not strum any multiple note combinations. For the Gmaj7 chords, your left-hand 4th and 2nd fingers will need to get to the B and high E string tones, respectively. The single-note lick in measure 12 should be played entirely with the 2nd finger except for the E on the B string's 5th fret, which should be played with the 3rd finger. Shift your 2nd finger up a fret to play the C that begins measure 13. The 2nd finger should also perform all of the hammer-ons and pull-offs in measure 16.

TRACK 24

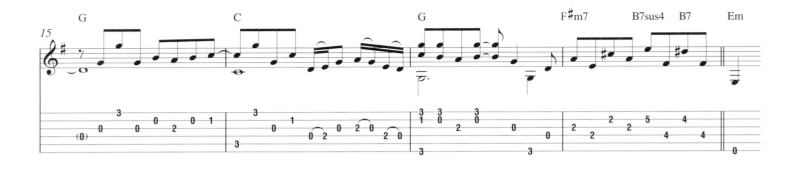

Bridge

This 10-measure section begins with the left-hand thumb fretting the chord roots on the low E string and the 2nd finger performing the hammer-on in measure 1. You'll need to add a 1st finger barre on the top two strings during the F chord as well. The picking should remain in keeping with the approach used throughout the song, with the thumb plucking the roots, and the index, middle, and ring fingers taking the top three strings. During measure 6 (Fmaj7), use your 1st finger to play the root on the low E string, your 3rd finger to perform the G string hammer-on, and your 2nd finger to play the C on the B string.

TRACK 25

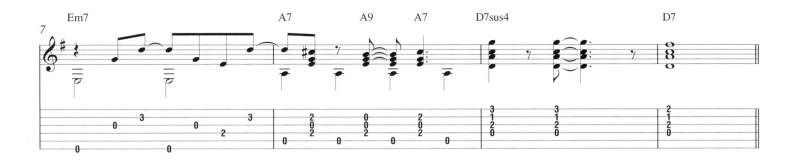

Outro

"You've Got a Friend" ends by returning to the instrumental motif first heard in the intro and at the conclusion of the choruses. Taylor's part is played in identical fashion to those earlier iterations; the fingerings are the same, as is the picking arrangement used by the right hand. Keep your left-hand fingers as arched as possible to ensure that all the strings ring freely throughout the excerpt.

TRACK 26

Deep River Blues

By Doc Watson

Traditional
Arranged and Adapted by Doc Watson

Copyright © 1964 (Renewed) Hillgreen Music
All Rights Reserved   Used by Permission

The greatly influential guitarist Doc Watson, now nearing 90 years of age, has been known primarily for his flat-picking prowess throughout his lengthy career. On "Deep River Blues," Watson's adaptation of an old-time traditional song of the south, he eschews the familiar flat pick and instead plays with his fingers in the style of Merle Travis, his contemporary and peer. Doc usually used "ring" style picks on his thumb and index finger to play this song, given him a brighter tone than bare flesh would produce, but you can play it however you choose. The right-hand thumb and index finger are the only fingers employed. Doc also rests the lower part of his palm on the strings gently, near the bridge, creating a slightly muffled tone throughout the song and affording him a sturdy, balanced picking base from which to work.

Verse (Part 1)

"Deep River Blues" is a simple song structurally and harmonically. It's 16 measures long and is basically a I–IV–V progression with a few passing notes thrown in as well as the tonic diminished chord (E°7), a commonly encountered sound in popular songs of the early part of the 20th century. However, there is a deceptively complex guitar technique at work here, and the task of pulling this one off with the confident, relaxed, breezy, and soulful air of the master is a daunting one. Doc's Travis picking approach seems simple on the surface, but the actual execution can be anything but. The thumb maintains a steady quarter note throughout the song as it alternates between the roots of the chords (on the low E and A strings) and (usually) the 3rds and 5ths on the D string. Watson says jokingly that he just played the thumb parts for about ten years before adding in the higher notes, but it's not such a bad idea at all. Try playing through the two verse excerpts by hitting only the quarter notes on the low strings with your thumb.

Back so soon? That wasn't ten years…I hope. Anyway, now it's time to add the upper notes played by the index finger. Measures 1 and 5 in the following example are particularly instructive, so let's take a moment to examine each in detail, as they'll help set the template for the rest of the song. In measure 1, your thumb will play the low E and D strings exclusively, alternating between the root and 3rd of the E7 chord on each quarter note. At the same time, your index finger will play the G, B, and high E string notes. Take a moment to play the phrase on the top three strings with this finger. The left-hand setup has the 2nd finger on the D string and the 3rd, 1st, and 4th fingers on the G, B, and high E strings, respectively. Ready for the next step? Put both hands together and play the measure over and over very slowly, without moving on, until you can pull it off smoothly and confidently with no hitches in either the picking or the rhythm.

Measure 5 is actually easier to play, but it's another pattern that pops up throughout the song in one form or another and is worth a closer look. Once again the thumb will play the quarter note roots (and the 5th) on the low E, A, and D strings. The index finger plucks only the B and high E strings in this measure and doesn't enter until the "2-and." In fact, the index finger only plays the off-beats here and doesn't ever pluck simultaneously with the thumb as it does on three separate occasions in measure 1. Still, practice this one until it's second nature as well.

Now add the rest of the excerpt a measure at a time. The picking arrangement in measure 2 follows that of the opening measure; shift your left hand so that your 1st and 2nd fingers play the 5th fret notes and your 3rd and 4th fingers play the 6th fret notes. On the 2nd beat of measure 3, pluck the G and high E strings together and slide from the 3rd to the 4th fret on both strings without picking again. Hammer-ons on the B string follow later in the measure and in measure 4 as well; each time your 2nd finger should come down hard enough to sound the C♯ without being plucked *at the same time* your thumb is plucking the D string. This is a technique we've already encountered in numerous songs earlier in these pages and can be tricky, as the timing of both hands has to be perfectly synchronized.

Finally, don't leave out the short little high E-string bends in measures 6 and 8; they should only raise the G a quarter tone and not all the way up to G♯.

Verse (Part II)

If you've worked your way patiently and diligently through the first half of the song, the rest shouldn't give you too many problems, as the techniques and fingerings are very much the same throughout. The key really is to take the song apart measure by measure, master each segment, and then piece it all back together one chunk at a time.

A few new wrinkles come up in the excerpt below. In measure 1, the thumb should play the E and D string notes, as already established, but the 2nd note here is on the "1-and" (not on beat 2), which is a minor deviation from the pattern. Consequently, the index finger will play two consecutive notes on beat 2 before order is then restored in the second half of the measure when we return to the alternating picking sequence of thumb, index finger, and then both fingers together on beat 4. The upper string hammer-ons, coinciding with thumb-plucked notes on the lower strings, return frequently throughout the excerpt as well. Notice how much easier it is to pull-off than hammer-on while plucking the bass notes; this technique appears in measures 4 and 6. There's also a nifty turnaround phrase in measures 5 and 6 that combines ascending bass notes (E–G#–A–A#–B) with melodic phrases on the upper strings; Watson returns frequently to this phrase, or a variation of it, throughout his many recorded versions of the song.

Turnaround Fill I

The first of two fills shown below extends the form of the song, as it begins on measure 15, runs into measure 16, and then adds a 17th measure to the total. Doc's playing all alone here, so he can do this when and if the mood strikes him. This fill is simply a slick pull-off lick on the bottom three strings; each pull-off should be initiated by the 2nd finger, moving to the 1st finger and the open string, or directly to the open string, as indicated in the notation and tablature. Be sure to pull down slightly as you pull-off to ensure that each unpicked note is heard clearly. In the final measure, use your index finger to strum the four-note chords on beat 2 and then return to the thumb-and-index finger plucking approach on beats 3 and 4.

TRACK 29

Turnaround Fill II

In our final example from "Deep River Blues," Doc plays a basic turnaround phrase that once again finds him altering the rhythmic arrangement slightly. The thumb will take the low E and D strings and the index finger the G and high E strings until beats 3 and 4 of measure 2, so each finger plays consecutive notes three separate times. During the final four eighth notes, the picking should be index finger, index finger, thumb, index finger. Fool around with the rhythm and feel of this phrase; it can work nicely at the end of any E blues chorus, regardless of style. Timeless and classic!

TRACK 30

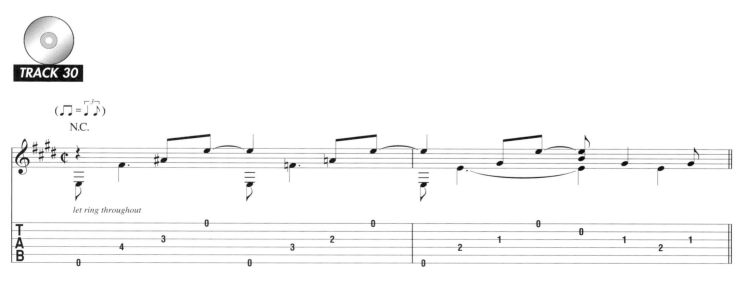

Tears in Heaven

By Eric Clapton
From *Rush* (1992)

Words and Music by Eric Clapton and Will Jennings

Copyright © 1992 by E.C. Music Ltd. and Blue Sky Rider Songs
All Rights for E.C. Music Ltd. Administered by Unichappell Music Inc.
All Rights for Blue Sky Rider Songs Administered by Irving Music, Inc.
International Copyright Secured   All Rights Reserved

Eric Clapton penned this tender and heartfelt song after the tragic accidental death of his young son, Conor, in 1991. It also figured prominently in his score for the 1992 film *Rush* and garnered three Grammy Awards (Song of the Year, Record of the Year, and Male Pop Vocal Performance) in 1993. A live version was included in his massively successful *MTV Unplugged* album as well. Clapton plays a nylon string acoustic on the original recording, as well as for the *Unplugged* version, but a steel string would work too. You can even play it on an electric with a pure, clean tone if you like, though the natural, woody sound of an acoustic is hard to duplicate unless you're playing a big, arch-top style hollowbody.

Intro

The roots of the chords on the A and low E string are plucked with the thumb, while the upper strings are mostly "grabbed" by the index finger, middle finger, and, when required, the ring finger. Eric uses his left-hand thumb to fret most of the low E string notes, which may take a little getting used to and be particularly challenging if your hands are on the small side (Stephen Stills uses the same technique on "Helplessly Hoping," as does John Mayer during "The Heart of Life," examined later in this book). As you work your way through the song, you will notice that, for the most part, you can fret these notes normally, with some small adjustment of the other fingers, if you choose. The hammer-on/pull-off move on the B string in measure 1, a motif that returns frequently, should be played with the 1st finger remaining in place at the 2nd fret while the 2nd finger does the work a fret above.

TRACK 31

Verse

The accompaniment to the verse is simple and straightforward, sticking to the techniques and fingerings employed during the intro.

TRACK 32

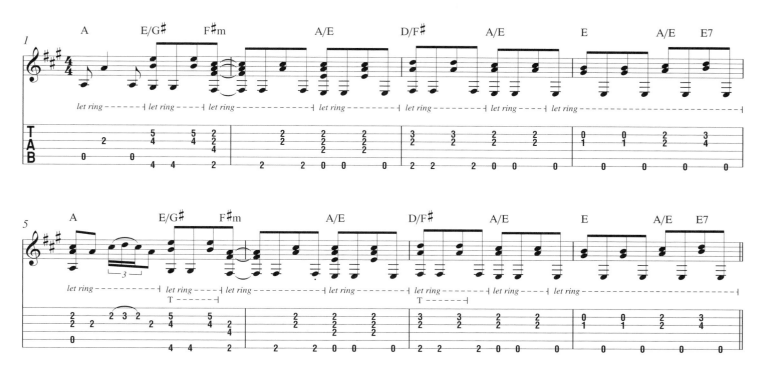

Chorus

"Tears in Heaven" doesn't actually have a proper "chorus" as much as a natural extension of the verse; the excerpt below begins with the lyric "I must be strong, and carry on." For the F#7 chord, leave the 1st finger in place, barring the strings at the 2nd fret. The B on beat 3 (G string, 4th fret) should be played by the 3rd finger, while the final note (C#) is taken by the 1st finger, still in the barre. In the final two measures, you can remain in place on a standard Bm7 barre chord fingering, simply adding in the low E string just before measure 6.

TRACK 33

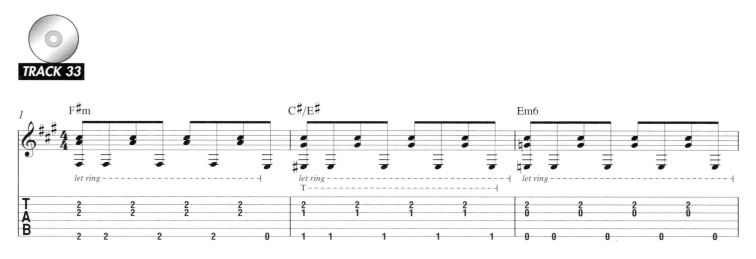

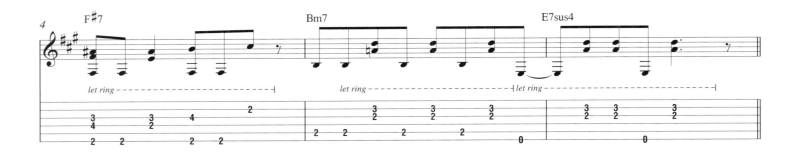

Bridge

"Tears in Heaven" modulates smoothly to the key of G in the bridge and then returns to the initial key (A) when it moves to the V chord (E) in the final measure. In this section, Clapton continues to use his left-hand thumb on the low E string but plays the 3rd fret G notes with his 2nd finger. The right-hand thumb should pluck only the low E and A strings. The middle finger should play all high E string notes as well as many of those on the B string. The index finger will take all the notes in between. For instance, each two-note grouping in measure 3 should be played by the index finger on the G string and the middle finger on the B string.

TRACK 34

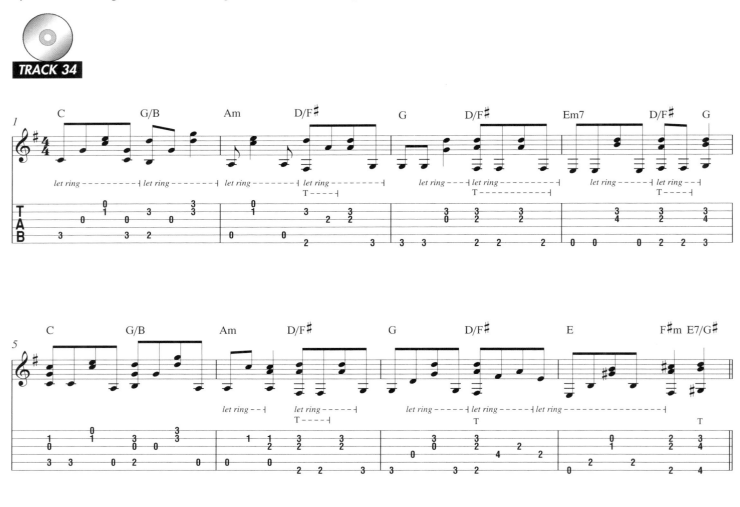

Ending

"Tears in Heaven" ends much as it begins, with a return to the opening motif and chord progression. Clapton puts a beautiful bow on the song with a single-note lick in the final measure using the thumb to pick each note save the hammer-on/pull-off executed with the left-hand 2nd finger. Barre the D, G, and B strings at the 2nd fret and stay there until the 3rd finger is used to slide up the G string from the 4th fret to the 6th fret. The last two notes should be played by the 2nd finger.

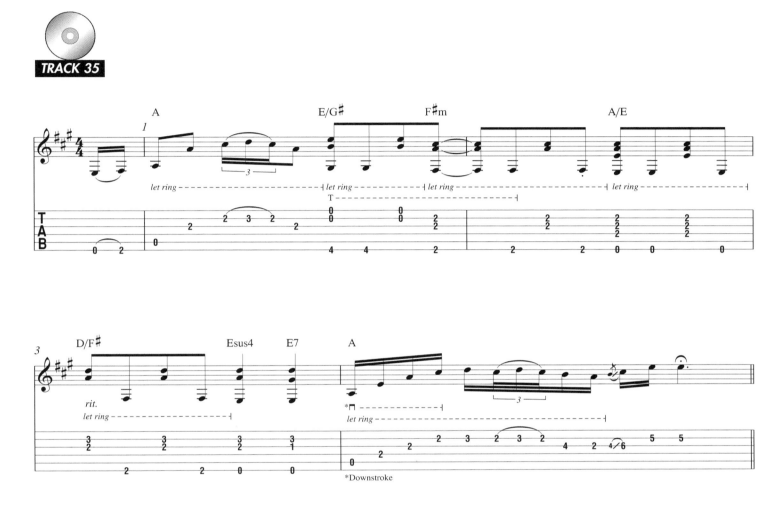

The Heart of Life

By John Mayer
From _Continuum_ (2006)

Words and Music by John Mayer

Copyright © 2006 Sony/ATV Music Publishing LLC and Specific Harm Music
All Rights Administered by Sony/ATV Music Publishing LLC, 8 Music Square West, Nashville, TN 37203
International Copyright Secured   All Rights Reserved

Mega pop star and Stratocaster virtuoso John Mayer has always had a kinder, gentler side. On this melodic, thoughtful tune from his Grammy Award-winning album _Continuum_, Mayer returns as he often does to his acoustic roots, singing sweetly and providing his own accompaniment. Although there are electric guitar overdubs, the song's foundation lies in his simple (but certainly not easy) steel string chordal riffs. Mayer's strong and propulsive rhythmic approach keeps the song moving along nicely—indeed, the bass and drums are never missed. This is a musician with the rare ability to tell a story and create a world of refined sound and expression all by himself. He sounds great fronting a band and cranking the amps up too, but a song like this impresses with its transparency, vulnerability and bare emotion. Each string is tuned down a half-step (E♭–A♭–D♭–G♭–B♭–E♭, low to high), so be sure to make this adjustment if you're going to play along with the recording.

Intro

Mayer uses his left-hand thumb to play low E string notes on many of the songs in his repertoire, and "The Heart of Life" is no exception. As in "Tears in Heaven," you may need to work on this technique for a while if it's new to you or especially if your hands are on the smaller side. In combination with the idiosyncratic picking approach used here, it's likely you'll need to practice the opening measure for a while before you're ready to tackle the rest of the song. In fact, much of the technical demands for both hands are revealed in this measure, so once you're comfortable, proceeding through the rest of the tune won't be nearly as difficult. Throughout the song, the right-hand thumb plays all of the low E and A string notes, with the index finger plucking the B string on beats 1 and 3. On beats 2 and 4, the thumb plucks the muted roots while the index finger plays the two-note combinations above simultaneously with a downward flick across the D and G strings. It's a very personal approach and one that's more than a little awkward at first, so be prepared to put some practice time in, working slowly and patiently until it begins to feel more natural to you.

Let's take a moment to discuss the chord fingerings on the upper strings. For the D chord, use your 3rd, 2nd, and 1st fingers on the D, G, and B strings, respectively, adding your 4th finger to the B string's 12th fret in measure 2. The same fingering applies to the G chord in measure 6. The Bm chord is played with the 1st finger barring the G and B strings at the 7th fret, the 3rd finger playing the D string, and the 4th finger grabbing the 10th fret A on the B string in measure 4. The F♯m is played in similar fashion, while the D/F♯ uses the 1st and 2nd fingers on the G and B strings. Leave them in place, but extend the 1st finger into a 2nd fret barre during the A chord at the end of the intro.

TRACK 36

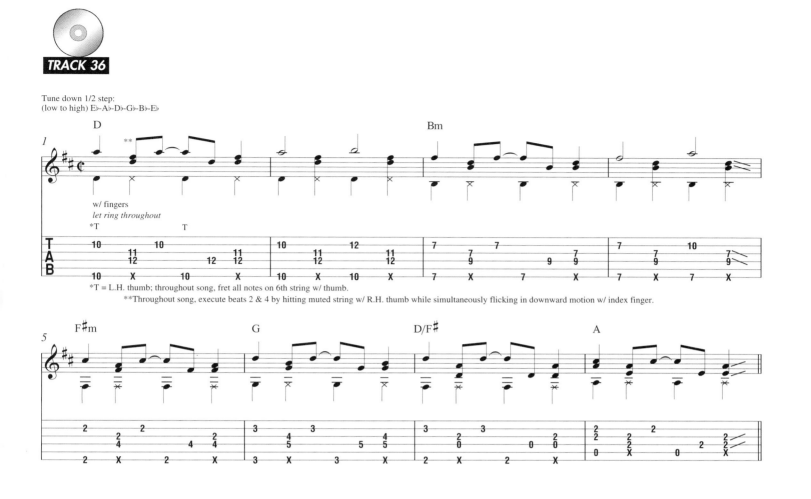

Tune down 1/2 step:
(low to high) E♭-A♭-D♭-G♭-B♭-E♭

w/ fingers
let ring throughout

*T = L.H. thumb; throughout song, fret all notes on 6th string w/ thumb.
**Throughout song, execute beats 2 & 4 by hitting muted string w/ R.H. thumb while simultaneously flicking in downward motion w/ index finger.

Verse/Variation

The riff above continues through the verse after Mayer's vocal entrance, but an important and challenging variation on the first four measures is introduced. Begin in the same fashion, but play the three-note grouping on beat 2 of the 2nd measure with your 3rd, 2nd, and 4th fingers on the D, G, and B strings, respectively. The C♯ on beat 3 (high E string, 9th fret) should be played by reaching back with the 1st finger, while the chord on beat 4 should be played with the 2nd, 3rd, and 1st fingers on the G, B, and high E strings, respectively. In measure 4, use your 3rd, 1st, and 4th fingers on the D, G, and B strings, respectively, on beat 2. The C♯ on beat 3 is played by the 3rd finger, while the chord on beat 4 should be played with a 1st finger barre. The right-hand approach remains consistent with the technique established in the introduction.

TRACK 37

Tune down 1/2 step:
(low to high) E♭-A♭-D♭-G♭-B♭-E♭

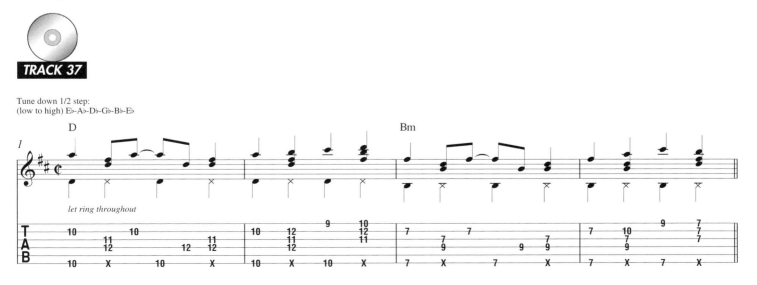

let ring throughout

Chorus

During this section, as in the rest of the song, the right hand keeps alternating between thumb-plucked bass notes and the combination of the thumb on muted notes and index finger strums on beats 2 and 4. The left-hand thumb continues to play all the low E string notes. For the A chords, use your 3rd, 2nd, and 1st fingers, adding the 4th finger to the G string's 7th fret on beat 3. The D chord is played with the 1st finger spanning the 5th fret to get to both the root and the E on beat 3, while the 3rd finger plays the 7th fret notes. Play the G and Gsus2 chords with your 2nd finger on the B string and your 1st and 3rd fingers taking the 2nd and 4th fret notes on the G string, respectively. Simply slide the thumb down a fret to play the root of the D/F♯ in measures 12 and 14. The chorus concludes by returning to the figure used in both the intro and verse.

TRACK 38

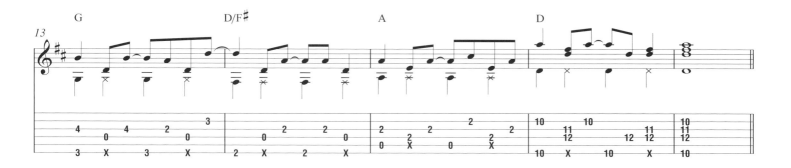

Outro Excerpt

"The Heart of Life" ends with a fade as Mayer lays soulful electric licks on top of the acoustic phrase below. The open A and G strings remain consistent in this riff, while the notes on the D and B strings track the A Mixolydian mode (A–B–C#–D–E–F#–G) up and down the neck. When the two notes on these strings are on the same fret, use your left-hand 1st and 2nd fingers on the D and B strings, respectively. Reverse the fingers, so the 2nd finger is on the D string and the 1st finger is on the B string, for each combination in which the lower note is one fret above the upper note (measures 2, 5, and 6). As the song fades away, Mayer moves as high as the 19th fret (not shown) to play the F# on the B string and A on the D string, duplicating the earlier measures an octave higher. The bottom of the right-hand thumb, where it meets the palm, is used to slightly muffle the open A string intermittently throughout the riff.

TRACK 39

Tune down 1/2 step:
(low to high) Eb-Ab-Db-Gb-Bb-Eb

Classical Gas

By Mason Williams
From *The Mason Williams Phonograph Record* (1968)

Music by Mason Williams

© 1967, 1968 Weems Music Co.
© Renewed 1995, 1996 Weems Music Co.
All Rights Reserved   Used by Permission

Our final song is truly a warhorse—perhaps *the* classic fingerpicking tune—and a staple of countless acoustic players the world over. It's heavily requested by both students and listeners and deserves a place in your repertoire, particularly if you're a gigging musician. Trust me, if you're a performing acoustic guitarist, you *will* be asked to play this one eventually. The guitarist and composer, Mason Williams, a multi-talent who also wrote comic sketches for the Smothers Brothers and *Saturday Night Live* and once appeared on television playing a clear plexiglass guitar filled with water and goldfish, won Grammy Awards for both composing and performing this song. "Classical Gas" is in A minor and uses open strings extensively, as well as many familiar left-hand chord shapes. Play it on a nylon string guitar if at all possible; it works on steel string and even electric, but you'll lose a lot of the "classical" and Spanish flavors that make the song so appealing to so many.

Intro

This section is played in *tempo rubato* (literally, "robbed time"), meaning that the beat is not strictly followed and each phrase and measure is allowed to proceed at the performer's chosen pace. You may linger on a note or move through a passage quickly at your own discretion. Be sure to give a listen to the original recording if you can to hear the way Mason Williams plays it. Take note of the *fermatas* (the upside down semi-circle and dot above the staff) in measures 8 and 11 as well; these indicate pauses in which the note or chord is held as long as the performer desires.

Play this intro by staying strictly in 1st position. Each G on the low E string's 3rd fret is played by the 3rd finger. The D notes on the B string in measure 10 should be played with the 4th finger, while the 3rd finger plays the root of the C chord on the A string. The squiggly vertical lines indicate a downwards strum that's dragged ever-so-slightly so that the sounding of the strings is somewhat staggered. Otherwise, the left-hand thumb should play the low E and A string notes while the index and middle fingers pluck the G and B string tones. The double-stop at the start of measure 10 should be "pinched" with the thumb and ring finger.

TRACK 40

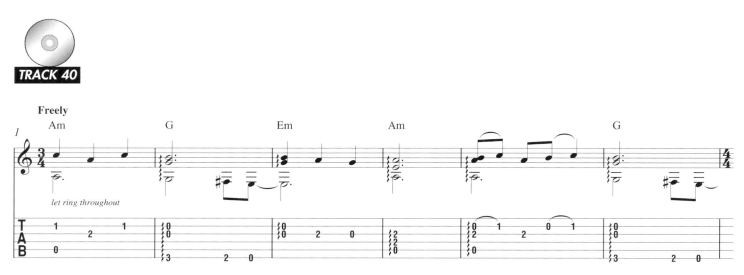

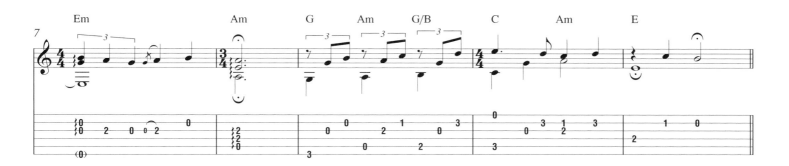

Main Riff and Extension

In this section, the time and beat is strictly established, but much of the material (until the 4th ending) has been already encountered in the intro. Take care to play each 2nd fret G string note with your 3rd finger so that you are able to smoothly return to the Am shapes (with the 2nd finger on the D string's 2nd fret) throughout the song. The picking here should follow the earlier arrangement, using primarily the thumb, index, and middle fingers but adding the ring finger to pick the high E string notes. In the final measure, the thumb strikes the low E string while the high E string notes may be played with the index finger alone or by alternating between the index and middle fingers.

One of the biggest "non-guitar" related challenges of "Classical Gas" is the numerous changes of time signature (4/4 to 2/4) and meter (4/4 to 6/8). In the former case, you are simply lopping off beats from a given measure. In the latter, the basic pulse changes, so that the eighth notes in 4/4 become the new beat (try counting this shift as "1-and-2-and-3-and-4-and 1-2-3-4-5-6," with every number and word given exactly equal duration). Whatever you do, don't guess with this stuff! Take the time to listen to the recording and COUNT your way through each phrase. Learn the changes and play them with confidence rather than guesswork and rough approximations.

TRACK 41

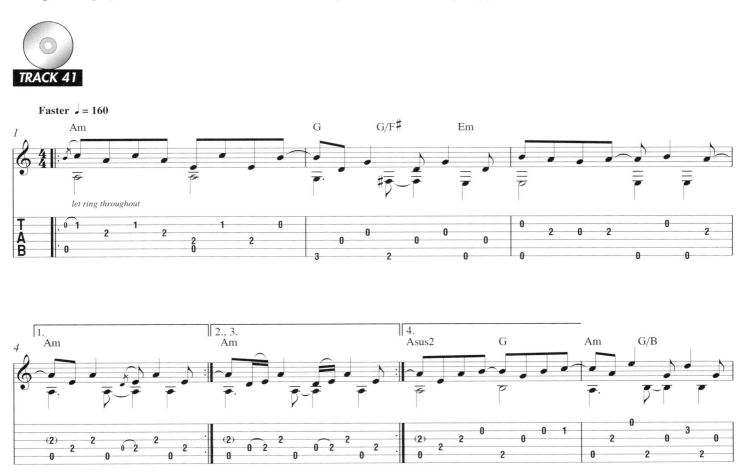

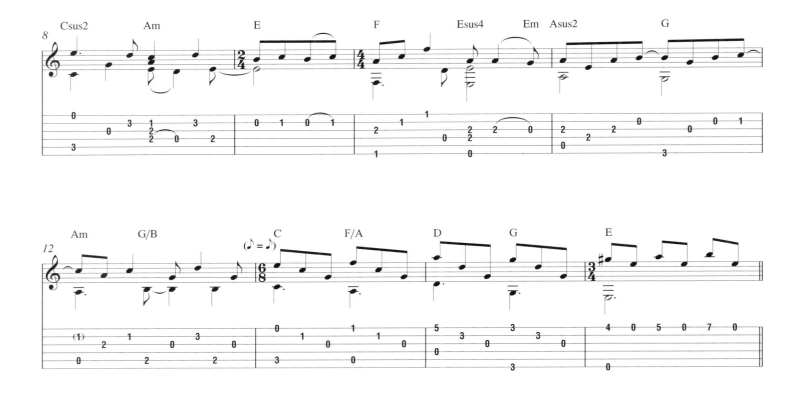

Riff II with Coda

This section follows the main riff and returns after Riff III (shown on page 54), when you play it again (but with a slightly different ending arpeggio) and then proceed to the "ending riff" that follows.

The left-hand fingerings in this section are a bit tricky, so take your time learning each measure. The 4th finger is used to play all 8th fret notes in the example. In measure 2, your 1st finger continues to play the A on the low E string's 5th fret, while your 3rd and 4th fingers take the 7th fret notes on the G and B strings. The 2nd finger will reach back and grab the 5th fret high E string notes as needed. The C, F, and B♭ chords in measure 7 are played with traditional barre chord shapes. Watch out for the 5/4 measure here! This is a tough rhythmic passage, so be sure to count your way through it.

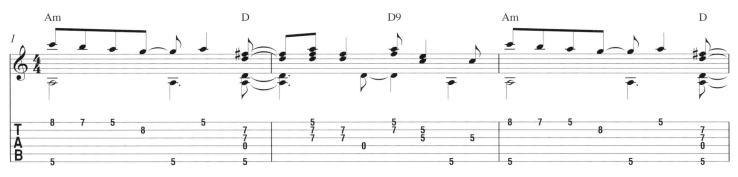

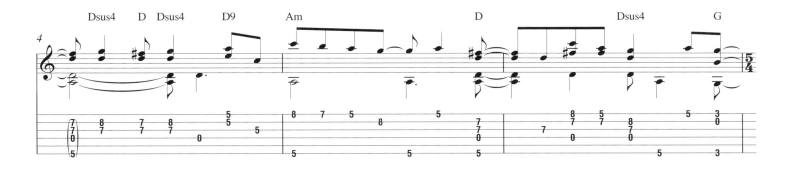

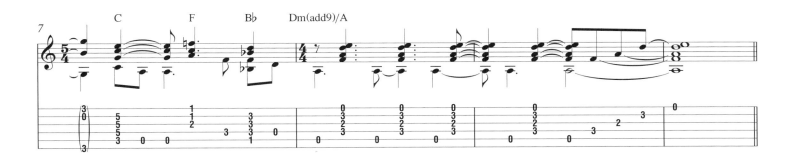

Riff III

The excerpt below follows the punchy interlude led by the brass section and begins at the 1:33 mark on the original recording. Much of it can be played in 1st position with your left hand moving through small variations on a standard A minor chord. Use your 3rd finger to slide up the G string at the end of measure 6 and play the 5th fret B string notes that follow with your 4th finger before returning to the A minor shape on the final beat of measure 7. The 4th finger should also play all of the 3rd fret B string notes (D) throughout the example. The picking will require the thumb, index, middle, and ring fingers in various combinations throughout the excerpt, with the ring finger mostly restricted to the high E string. In four-note passages on consecutive strings, such as those beginning on beat 3 of measures 1, 3, and 5, the ring finger should be used to pluck the B string as well.

TRACK 43

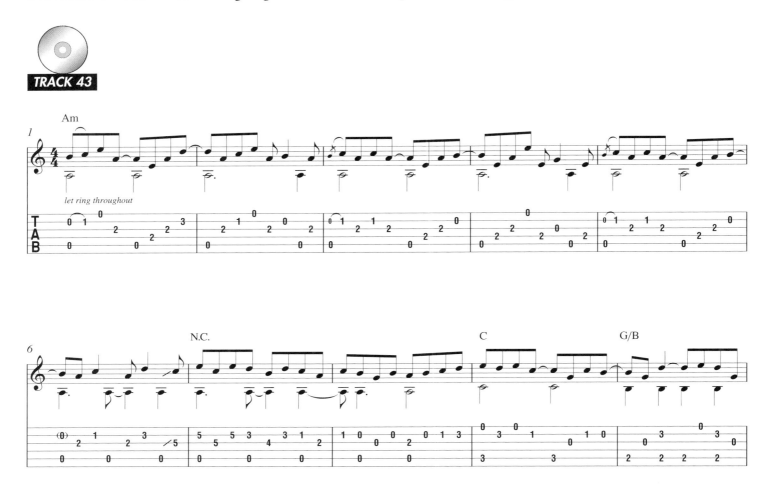

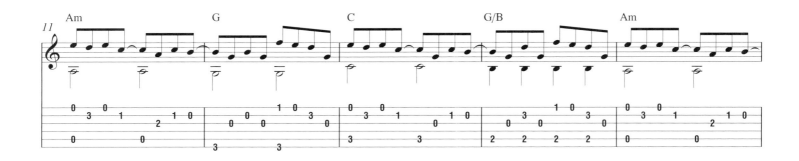

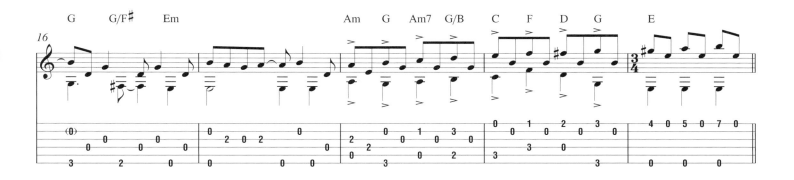

Ending Riff

The big "Classical Gas" finale immediately follows the Coda from Riff II and begins by returning to the main riff for both the 1st and 4th endings and then extends to the 2/4 measure played over the E chord. In the interest of space, these measures are not shown below, but you can find them easily enough by returning to the "main riff" example above if you need a bit of a refresher. We pick up the action with heavily accented chords in 1st position but quickly climb up the neck in measure 3. Watch out for the metric shifts in this section, which move first to 5/8 and then 6/8 for two measures, return to 5/8, and then conclude in 4/4. It's a whirlwind of rhythmic complexity that has to be counted out carefully to ensure accurate results.

The fingering in this section also merits careful examination. The 4th finger should play the 3rd fret notes in the first measure, as well as both the 7th fret high E string note (B) that ends measure 3 and the 5th fret note (A) that begins measure 4. The F chord in measure 6 is played with a conventional barre shape. Follow by using your 1st and 4th fingers to play the B♭ chord and then move your 1st finger up to the high E string's 1st fret as you reach the Dm(add9)/A chord. The Dadd9/A chord should be played with your 3rd, 1st, and 2nd fingers on the D, G, and B strings, respectively. The song ends with a simple A major chord played with a 1st finger barre.

TRACK 44

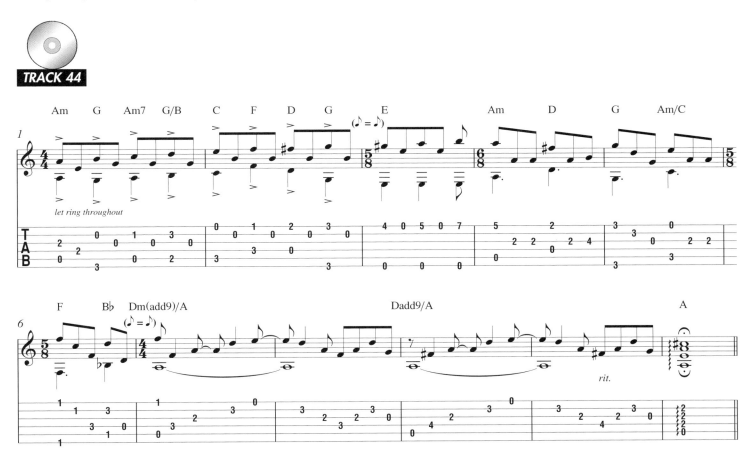

PLAY IT LIKE IT IS GUITAR
WITH TABLATURE
NOTE-FOR-NOTE TRANSCRIPTIONS

THE HOTTEST TAB SONGBOOKS AVAILABLE FOR GUITAR & BASS!

PLAY IT LIKE IT IS BASS
WITH TABLATURE
NOTE-FOR-NOTE TRANSCRIPTIONS

 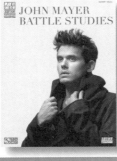

from

cherry lane
music company

Guitar Transcriptions

02501410	The Black Keys – Attack & Release	$19.99
02501500	The Black Keys – A Collection	$19.99
02500702	Best of Black Label Society	$22.95
02500842	Black Label Society – Mafia	$19.95
02500116	Black Sabbath – Riff by Riff	$14.95
02500882	Blues Masters by the Bar	$19.95
02500921	Best of Joe Bonamassa	$22.95
02501510	Joe Bonamassa Collection	$24.99
02501272	Bush – 16 Stone	$21.95
02500179	Mary Chapin Carpenter Authentic Guitar Style of	$16.95
02500336	Eric Clapton – Just the Riffs	$12.99
02501565	Coheed and Cambria – Year of the Black Rainbow	$19.99
02501439	David Cook	$22.99
02500684	Dashboard Confessional – A Mark • A Mission • A Brand • A Scar	$19.95
02500689	Dashboard Confessional – The Places You Have Come to Fear the Most	$17.95
02500843	Dashboard Confessional – The Swiss Army Romance	$17.95
02501481	Brett Dennen – So Much More	$19.99
02506878	John Denver Anthology for Easy Guitar Revised Edition	$15.95
02506901	John Denver Authentic Guitar Style	$14.95
02500984	John Denver – Folk Singer	$19.95
02506928	John Denver – Greatest Hits for Fingerstyle Guitar	$14.95
02500632	John Denver Collection Strum & Sing Series	$9.95
02501448	Best of Ronnie James Dio	$22.99
02500607	The Best of Dispatch	$19.95
02500198	Best of Foreigner	$19.95
02500990	Donavon Frankenreiter	$19.95
02501242	Guns N' Roses – Anthology	$24.95
02506953	Guns N' Roses – Appetite for Destruction	$22.95
02501286	Guns N' Roses Complete, Volume 1	$24.95
02501287	Guns N' Roses Complete, Volume 2	$24.95
02506211	Guns N' Roses – 5 of the Best, Vol. 1	$12.95
02506975	Guns N' Roses – GN'R Lies	$19.95
02500299	Guns N' Roses – Live Era '87-'93 Highlights	$24.95
02501193	Guns N' Roses – Use Your Illusion I	$24.99
02501194	Guns N' Roses – Use Your Illusion II	$24.95
02506325	Metallica – The Art of Kirk Hammett	$17.95
02500939	Hawthorne Heights – The Silence in Black and White	$19.95
02500458	Best of Warren Haynes	$22.95
02500476	Warren Haynes – Guide to Slide Guitar	$17.95

02500387	Best of Heart	$19.95
02500016	The Art of James Hetfield	$17.95
02500873	Jazz for the Blues Guitarist	$14.95
02500554	Jack Johnson – Brushfire Fairytales	$19.95
02500831	Jack Johnson – In Between Dreams	$19.95
02500653	Jack Johnson – On and On	$19.95
02501139	Jack Johnson – Sleep Through the Static	$19.95
02500858	Jack Johnson – Strum & Sing	$14.99
02501564	Jack Johnson – To the Sea	$19.99
02500380	Lenny Kravitz – Greatest Hits	$19.95
02500024	Best of Lenny Kravitz	$19.95
02500129	Adrian Legg – Pickin' 'n' Squintin'	$19.95
02500362	Best of Little Feat	$19.95
02501094	Hooks That Kill – The Best of Mick Mars & Mötley Crüe	$19.95
02500305	Best of The Marshall Tucker Band	$19.95
02501077	Dave Matthews Band – Anthology	$24.99
02501357	Dave Matthews Band – Before These Crowded Streets	$19.95
02501279	Dave Matthews Band – Crash	$19.95
02501266	Dave Matthews Band – Under the Table and Dreaming	$19.95
02500131	Dave Matthews/Tim Reynolds – Live at Luther College, Vol. 1	$19.95
02500611	Dave Matthews/Tim Reynolds – Live at Luther College, Vol. 2	$22.95
02501502	John Mayer – Battle Studies	$22.99
02500986	John Mayer – Continuum	$22.99
02500705	John Mayer – Heavier Things	$22.95
02500705	John Mayer – Heavier Things	$22.95
02500529	John Mayer – Room for Squares	$22.95
02506965	Metallica – ...And Justice for All	$22.99
02501267	Metallica – Death Magnetic	$24.95
02506210	Metallica – 5 of the Best/Vol.1	$12.95
02506235	Metallica – 5 of the Best/Vol. 2	$12.95
02500070	Metallica – Garage, Inc.	$24.95
02507018	Metallica – Kill 'Em All	$19.99
02501232	Metallica – Live: Binge & Purge	$19.95
02501275	Metallica – Load	$24.95
02501195	Metallica – Metallica	$22.95
02501297	Metallica – ReLoad	$24.95
02507019	Metallica – Ride the Lightning	$19.95
02500279	Metallica – S&M Highlights	$24.95
02500638	Metallica – St. Anger	$24.95
02500577	Molly Hatchet – 5 of the Best	$9.95
02501529	Monte Montgomery Collection	$24.99
02500846	Best of Steve Morse Band and Dixie Dregs	$19.95

02500765	Jason Mraz – Waiting for My Rocket to Come	$19.95
02501324	Jason Mraz – We Sing, We Dance, We Steal Things.	$22.99
02500448	Best of Ted Nugent	$19.95
02500707	Ted Nugent – Legendary Licks	$19.95
02500844	Best of O.A.R. (Of a Revolution)	$22.95
02500348	Ozzy Osbourne – Blizzard of Ozz	$19.95
02501277	Ozzy Osbourne – Diary of a Madman	$19.95
02507904	Ozzy Osbourne/Randy Rhoads Tribute	$22.95
02500524	The Bands of Ozzfest	$16.95
02500680	Don't Stop Believin': The Steve Perry Anthology	$22.95
02500025	Primus Anthology – A-N (Guitar/Bass)	$19.95
02500091	Primus Anthology – O-Z (Guitar/Bass)	$19.95
02500468	Primus – Sailing the Seas of Cheese	$19.95
02500875	Queens of the Stone Age – Lullabies to Paralyze	$24.95
02500608	Queens of the Stone Age – Songs for the Deaf	$19.95
02500659	The Best of Bonnie Raitt	$24.95
02501268	Joe Satriani	$22.95
02501299	Joe Satriani – Crystal Planet	$24.95
02500306	Joe Satriani – Engines of Creation	$22.95
02501205	Joe Satriani – The Extremist	$22.95
02507029	Joe Satriani – Flying in a Blue Dream	$22.95
02501155	Joe Satriani – Professor Satchafunkilus and the Musterion of Rock	$24.95
02500544	Joe Satriani – Strange Beautiful Music	$22.95
02500920	Joe Satriani – Super Colossal	$22.95
02506959	Joe Satriani – Surfing with the Alien	$19.95
02500560	Joe Satriani Anthology	$24.99
02501255	Best of Joe Satriani	$19.95
02501238	Sepultura – Chaos A.D.	$19.95
02500188	Best of the Brian Setzer Orchestra	$19.95
02500985	Sex Pistols – Never Mind the Bollocks, Here's the Sex Pistols	$19.95
02501230	Soundgarden – Superunknown	$19.95
02500956	The Strokes – Is This It	$19.95
02501586	The Sword – Age of Winters	$19.99
02500799	Tenacious D	$19.95
02501035	Tenacious D – The Pick of Destiny	$19.95
02501263	Tesla – Time's Making Changes	$19.95
02501147	30 Easy Spanish Guitar Solos	$14.99
02500561	Learn Funk Guitar with Tower of Power's Jeff Tamelier	$19.95
02501440	Derek Trucks – Already Free	$24.99
02501007	Keith Urban – Love, Pain & The Whole Crazy Thing	$24.95
02500636	The White Stripes – Elephant	$19.95
02501095	The White Stripes – Icky Thump	$19.95
02500583	The White Stripes – White Blood Cells	$19.95
02501092	Wilco – Sky Blue Sky	$22.95
02500431	Best of Johnny Winter	$19.95
02500949	Wolfmother	$22.95
02500199	Best of Zakk Wylde	$22.99
02500700	Zakk Wylde – Legendary Licks	$19.95

Bass Transcriptions

02501108	Bass Virtuosos	$19.95
02500117	Black Sabbath – Riff by Riff Bass	$17.95
02506966	Guns N' Roses – Appetite for Destruction	$19.95
02501522	John Mayer Anthology for Bass, Vol. 1	$24.99
02500639	Metallica – St. Anger	$19.95
02500771	Best of Rancid for Bass	$17.95
02501120	Best of Tower of Power for Bass	$19.95
02500317	Victor Wooten Songbook	$22.95

Transcribed Scores

02500424	The Best of Metallica	$24.95
02500883	Mr. Big – Lean into It	$24.95

See your local music dealer or contact:

cherry lane
music company

EXCLUSIVELY DISTRIBUTED BY

HAL•LEONARD CORPORATION
7777 W. BLUEMOUND RD. P.O. BOX 13819 MILWAUKEE, WI 53213

Prices, contents, and availability subject to change without notice.

0211